WE'LL BE WITH YOU

Every step along the way, since 1863

Best Wishes

Brian Darling

Brian Darling

PublishNation
www.publishnation.co.uk

This book is dedicated to the memory of my Nephew, Duncan Darling who sadly passed away on Sunday 20th September 2020.

Acknowledgements

To the boys and girls in Block 21. The old brigade, Ade, Simon, Steve and T4 and the young ones, Max, Gina, Ross, Laura, Emma, Joe and John and for my sons Dan and Tom. Thank you for your friendship and company.

Also thanks to Emma for her fabulous work on the book covers, for Tom for managing the Instagram account and Mark Taylor and Infogel for a variety of statistical data. Further thanks to my various proof readers for whom beer will be your reward.

Special mention and thanks goes to my generous lead sponsors who helped maximize the contribution to the charity:

Martin and Alice O'Shea
Carl Cooper
Karl Bamford
Andy Slee

Registered Charity Number 1168463

The Macari Centre was established by the Macari Foundation in 2016 and offers direct access accommodation for people who are sleeping rough on the Streets of Stoke on Trent. The Centre offers warmth, safety and shelter to those who find themselves sleeping rough, offering hospitality and care and reducing poverty for some of the most vulnerable people in our society. They provide food and a bed with the help and support from a dedicated team.

"Save me my place on the Boothen,
Picture it just like it was,
Give me a shirt forever,
On the steps where I used to dream,
In that corrugated shed of a fortress,
Where the crowd became part of the team".

Extract from YOU, ME AND DELILAH, J Bennett.

PROLOGUE

This book is all about the experience of celebrating success to the full while also enduring inevitable, heart breaking disappointment. They are close neighbours. As a Stoke City fan for almost fifty years I am well practised in both departments. My club embraces Newton's law of gravity, "what goes up, must come down."

Stoke City became an established Premier League club in 2008 and remained for a decade, with wealthy, generous UK owners, playing in front of capacity crowds every week. They had international players from Austria, Switzerland, Spain, USA, France, Germany all the home nations as well as from the African continent and beyond; all on fully leaded Premier League contracts.

For a dozen years, there had been just two managers of the club spanning the Premier League years 2008 to 2018. The long-standing Tony Pulis for seven years who guided the club to the elite division and instilled an iron backbone. He gave us a Wembley final appearance in 2011 and a European adventure. He was replaced by Mark Hughes and in almost five years at the club achieved three consecutive ninth place finishes and brought back the style of players to Stoke City we hadn't seen grace the top league in the world since the 1970's; Alan Hudson's era.

Times changed and between January 2018 and November 2019, just twenty-two months, there have been five managers. A damaging relegation season in 2018 was a massive wakeup call but *no one* woke up and a new relegation battle was underway in the Championship in 2019/20.

We had spent well over £200m on transfer fees during Premier League years and toward the end of that era made two record signings, both for £18m. These players have appeared on just handfuls of occasions and in common with some other notable big money signings they have betrayed our Club, with their appalling behaviour, disgraceful attitude and total lack of commitment. They subsequently became valueless within a year!

These signings were gambles that backfired. When Stoke City signed Alan Hudson from Chelsea, their best player, in 1974 for £240,000, it was also a record signing. This wasn't a gamble in the slightest.

With unrest in the squad and turbulence and volatility in the management and coaching staff, even the loyal fan base became divided.

From ninth in the Premier League in March 2017 to bottom of the Championship in eighteen months was a devastating fall from grace. Could the decline be arrested in a way that neither Sunderland or Bolton had been able to achieve in recent seasons?

Would the players be up for the fight? Some wouldn't. But some would, a new cohort playing literally for their lives, their reputation and their entire future in the beautiful game.

Much had changed. Some things hadn't. The loyal support for the Club remains, it groans and mithers, but is always there come rain or shine. It's always been the same. We are always there, *no matter what*. Waiting, hoping and praying that the good times will return.

We are lucky. We still have generous, loyal, proud local owners who remain serial investors in the club. The Coates family who have been in situ for fifteen years have also seen it all. We continue to rely on them as they help provide new pieces of the puzzle. All we need to do is find the solution to the riddle.

In over a dozen years the owners have frozen season ticket prices, recognising the local demographics in Stoke on Trent and knowing the value and power of a full stadium. I live in Northampton where Northampton Town, The Cobblers, play nearby at Sixfields Stadium. They were promoted from League

Two to League One this year and a season ticket there is comfortably more expensive than my seat in the Boothen End at Stoke City and has been throughout our Premier League years.

Sometimes, even when you possess all the cards; all the jigsaw pieces to complete the picture and then exploit the opportunity to take charge and dominate, it's still not possible. Uncontrollable things happen.

In March 2020, there was another threat to football, to humanity. Covid-19 swept across the world in a global pandemic never witnessed before by anyone alive on the planet.

Can we, and will we prevail?

We always do. We evolve, become more agile and we adapt. As we change and win the war against this silent, invisible, deadly plague, there will be a new normal.

"We'll be with you, every step along the way". Our club anthem, has never been so poignant. It's time for togetherness, not division. It's time for strength and resolve, not weakness or submission.

We *will* prevail. And we *will* be stronger having faced the challenge.

We know and believe that United Strength is Stronger

VIS UNITA FORTIOR

CHAPTER ONE

26th January 2016.

Joe Allen stepped up to take the penalty.

We stood motionless, shoulder to shoulder, waiting, hoping, dreaming. Time was almost frozen. The anticipation was both exhilarating and terrifying at the same time. Yet we were absolutely captivated, nothing capable of distracting us from this moment. And it was Joe, but not at this stage *our* Joe Allen, who had the honour.

It had already been a breathless evening in the cool, dry floodlit stadium. We had won at Anfield for the first time in fifty-six years and deservedly so. Scores were level, 1 - 1 on aggregate and remained that way through extra time.

Earlier, before Joe's final kick of the evening, penalties by Walters, Whelan, Afellay, Shaqiri and the on loan Van Ginkel had taken us to a 5 - 4 lead in the shootout. At that point it was sudden death and I stood, arm round my son Dan with a Wembley final beckoning. The penalties were being taken in front of the packed away end, full of anticipation but helpless in that moment. We were on the brink of a Cup Final at Wembley. This felt like the tensest moment in all the forty-five years I had been following Stoke City.

Lucas had other ideas and scored his penalty to equalise for Liverpool to make it five each. It's still a sudden death situation. Marc Muniesa, our passionate, talented Spanish defender stepped up and struck the ball solidly. Mignolet, the Liverpool keeper dived the right way and instead of a rippling net, the ball bounced off his legs and forward to safety. The realisation seemed to hit the traveling Stoke fans first. Mignolet was in raptures and Klopp celebrated on the touch line.

So, Joe stepped forward, focused, purposeful, confident, head down and balanced. He struck the ball firmly, the sound of the contact reverberated. Within a fraction of a second later, with our keeper helplessly on his backside, looking back over his shoulder having been sent the wrong way, the ball hit the net.

The ball striking the net made its distinctive and unique sound. Usually it's a truly wonderful and exhilarating sound, but not on this occasion. Now it was instantly replaced with a deafening roar from the Anfield faithful. One of the few moments during the evening the home fans were heard.

We hung our heads. It was over. It was brave, but it was over. In the same moment, I was both incredibly proud while feeling physically sick.

We had dominated the game at Anfield. Against the odds, we had deservedly triumphed for the first time in more than half a century. The only thing lacking was the second crucial goal to win the game in the ninety minutes and avoid extra time and after that, the binary experience of a penalty shootout - either magical or horrifying.

We had lost the first leg at home 1 - 0, when we all felt, to give us a realistic chance, we needed to take an advantage to Anfield for the second leg. The anticipation of the second leg wasn't as charged as usual because we knew the only route to prevailing in this two-legged tie, was to win on the night, at Anfield.

We hoped, but maybe didn't truly believe that it would be possible. The Stoke City team were true gladiators that night, defending like lions when necessary. Going forward, it was clear the doubts that may have been entertained within the raucous away support didn't exist within the team. They were terrific and reminded me of the flair and talent of the Stoke City team of the mid 1970's, when I witnessed for the first time the magic of how Jimmy Greenhoff and Alan Hudson combined.

Now it was Arnautovic and Bojan who were calling the tune. We also had grafters in our team, players whose efforts paved the way for our playmakers. Our bench was strong and Xherdan Shaqiri, our Swiss International winger waited in the wings for his chance to express himself when the time came.

Our goal came from Arnautovic, finding space in the box as Bojan intelligently threaded a pass to him from a wide position. He scored expertly at the near post leaving the Kop silent in their seats. In the lower tier of the Anfield Road end no seats were occupied as Stoke fans enjoyed a vigorous, lengthy celebration.

To win on the night at Anfield was fantastic in itself, but it would only be good enough to reach the final and face Manchester City at Wembley if we came through the thirty minutes of extra time and penalties (if required). It's almost unbelievable that Liverpool resorted to cynical fouling tactics in desperation to stay in the tie. Several were committed by the reckless Flanagan. By the time Bojan was subbed and both Arnautovic and Charlie Adam (only a recent substitute himself) had to leave the field with injuries, Flanagan should have been dismissed. The loss of these players deprived us of some of our best penalty takers who were absent for the shootout.

Forgive me if this sounds bitter. Across the five decades I have been following Stoke City I have longed for a team to match and even surpass a Liverpool side at Anfield. However, after an emotional, stirring shootout Joe Allen, now Stoke City's Joe Allen, had sent Liverpool through to the final.

Penalties, as I move on to discuss a little later, were to become problematic for us.

I recall feeling similarly as drained on just one other occasion. Gillingham away in the second leg of the League One play- offs in 2000. We took a 3 - 2 lead to the Priestfield Stadium before ultimately losing 5 - 3 on aggregate having had two men sent off in another disastrously poor refereeing performance.

The lasting affects of the Liverpool encounter had long term impacts on the club and the fans, me included. Worse than that, it seemed to have a similar affect on the players.

The remainder of the season saw a mixed bag of results. We won five and lost seven of the last fifteen games, conceding thirty times. It had in many ways been a remarkable season. Memorable victories over Chelsea and Man Utd were eclipsed by a stunning performance and 2-0 win over Man City. This is widely regarded as the best performance in the top flight by a Stoke City team for decades with Arnautovic, Bojan and Shaqiri playing starring roles.

We had travelled to Everton over the Christmas period and spectacularly won a thriller 4 - 3. It was a game that swung both ways and required the level headed Arnautovic to score a dramatic ninety first minute penalty to seal the victory and the three points.

But while some performances were sprinkled with magic dust, others were ordinary at best and though we still finished in a very respectable ninth place above the likes of Chelsea - the cracks were beginning to become visible. Our minus fourteen goal difference was a statistic that didn't lie.

My belief is that the legacy of that night in Liverpool still haunts us. It represented the peak, the summit of our team's progression and it came at a price. A hugely expensive price.

It's true that there is a catalogue of reasons for our decline (which I will come onto at a later stage). It just felt that having reached this summit, a downward trajectory was now by far the most probable direction of travel.

CHAPTER TWO

Where and how it all fell apart, and kept falling apart.

First the headlines, then the story.

- In July 2015, Steven Nzonzi was sold to Sevilla for £7 million. He was never adequately replaced.

- During January 2016, Gianelli Imbula was signed for a record £18 million on a five and a half year contract. He played just twenty six times for the club.

- In March 2016, in form goalkeeper Jack Butland fractured his ankle playing for England.

Stoke City finished the season in ninth place in the Premier League

****

- In January 2017. Saido Berahino was signed for £12 million from West Brom on a five and a half year contract. The contract was eventually terminated after a series of serious misdemeanors.

Stoke City finished the season in thirteenth place in the Premier League

****

- In late July 2017, talisman Marco Arnautovic was sold to West Ham for £25 million. He was never adequately replaced.

- During August 2017, Kevin Wimmer was signed for £18 million on a five year contract. An inexplicable signing who has made only seventeen appearances.

Stoke finished the season in nineteenth place, second to bottom and were relegated from the Premier League

****

The Story.

If these headlines aren't upsetting enough, the story that unfolds will tip you over the edge.

My take on the story looks back as far as the Summer break following the end of the 2014/15 season.

We had barely finished celebrating the demolition of Liverpool in a thumping 6 - 1 home win. This was our largest margin of victory in a Premier League game and at the same time, the heaviest Premier League defeat *ever* suffered by Liverpool.

Even Steven Gerrard in his final game for his boyhood side couldn't inspire them and the truth is, it could have been far worse than the score line suggests. Stoke eased off in the second half having cruised to a 5 - 0 lead at half time, as our players left the field smiling and waving to fans at the interval.

In the second half, having allowed Gerrard to dance unchallenged into our box and score his consolation goal, we awoke again with Peter Crouch scoring a trade-mark header at the back post to restore our five goal advantage. This goal took Crouch to the record number of headed goals by any striker in

Premier League history, forty seven, surpassing the record previously held by Alan Shearer. With that number lifted to fifty three by the time Crouch retired, it's difficult to see it ever being overcome

Being greedy, I really wanted Stoke to score eight goals that day to finally erase the painful memory of the 8 - 0 thrashing handed out to us by Liverpool in the League Cup game in November 2000. For most of the match it looked perfectly likely we would match that feat!

While we were all celebrating and luxuriating in that final day victory over the Summer, the club allowed Steven Nzonzi to depart in search of European glory with Sevilla. The failing wasn't necessarily allowing Nzonzi to leave, it was the inability to tie him into a longer term contract that would have enabled us to at least achieve fair market value for his services rather than the £7 million we did actually receive.

This still became our record transfer receipt at the time, but his services were missed considerably more.

Nzonzi played one hundred and nine times for Stoke and quietly went about his business breaking up play and controlling the midfield. Yes, he had a short fuse and was prone to the odd sulk, but my, oh my, he did a sublime job for Stoke City. The £3 million spent on bringing him to the club in the first place was an amazing piece of business.

His goal against Liverpool on his final appearance, our fifth before half time, was exquisite. He gracefully strode through the Liverpool midfield and approaching the left corner of the box, opened his body to plant a curling twenty five yard screamer into the top right hand corner, with keeper Mignolet rooted to the spot.

He did move on to greater heights and now proudly possesses a UEFA Europa Cup winners medal and FIFA World Cup winners medal. He was a world class player.

Stoke never entirely replaced Steven Nzonzi. The truth is that it would have been a tough ask to do so. Even if a comparable player did exist and was available, the cost would have been astronomic. Evidence of his true career value was displayed when Roma paid Sevilla €30 million for him in August 2018.

Another notable departure from the club during the same transfer window was the popular Robert Huth. A no nonsense defender, hard as nails and effective in both boxes. He served the club for six years and had been on loan at Leicester City since January 2015. While on loan at Leicester, he was a key part of both their survival in the Premier League that season and their shock Premier League title winning squad in 2015/16. He had been carrying an injury and while that was a concern to Stoke, the new centre half pairing of Ryan Shawcross and Philipp Wollscheid was never as solid without Huth.

Stoke's 2015/16 season began with high levels of excitement and anticipation amongst fans, despite the regrettable departure of a couple of our favourite players. Pre-season included a wonderful trip to Cologne, really popular with fans and Dan and I thoroughly enjoyed beers, steak and football in the sun. An array of club flags were on display in the large square near to the imposing Gothic Cologne cathedral on match day and familiar songs were sung as we bathed in twenty eight degree sunshine.

The excitement grew as the season approached with news of the signing of Swiss winger, Xherdan Shaqiri for £12 million from Inter Milan who we had targeted for some time. At the time, this was Stoke's record signing and Shaqiri possessed a strong Curriculum Vitea having played for both Bayern Munich and Inter Milan before joining Stoke. The elegant Dutch midfielder Afellay also joined.

Although we lost on the opening day 1 - 0 at home to Liverpool, a stirring comeback from 2 - 0 down to draw at White Hart Lane lifted our spirits a week later. The Marc Muniesa song to the tune of La Bamba was born on that day and rang out for a full twenty minutes in the ground.

With just two points from five games (after the customary loss at Arsenal in early September) Stoke had made their worst start to a Premier League campaign.

This season was characterised by ups and downs. Importantly, Stoke gained early point hauls against sides in the bottom third of the table. The first win of the season was in our seventh match against Bournemouth at home in late September. This was rapidly followed by two 1 – 0 victories away at Aston Villa and then at Swansea.

Wins at home to Chelsea in both the League and League Cup ensured spirits remained high and December proved memorable with four wins. Three in the League and a League Cup Quarter Final victory at home to Sheffield Wednesday to earn the club a place in the Semi Finals of the League Cup for the first time since winning the competition in 1972.

The three League wins were outstanding. First Man City were annihilated at the Britannia. Arnautovic had become the talisman, top scorer and, combining with Shaqiri, scored twice. He should have completed his hat-trick before half time, the ball rebounding off the inside of the post with Joe Hart stranded. Man Utd fell to the same 2 - 0 score line on Boxing Day with both Arnautovic and Bojan on target. It's amazing to say it was almost a routine victory.

The final game of 2015 was away at Everton and in a ding-dong game that swung both ways. Stoke triumphed 4 – 3 in a hugely entertaining match. Arnautovic was again on target with a penalty in injury time to seal the win.

2015 had been littered with inconsistent performances and results and ended on a high after that special month in December. Every Stoke City fan celebrated this fabulous sequence of results.

January saw the inconsistency return and Stoke lost four of their first six games of the new year. This run included three consecutive 3 - 0 defeats. Stoke also met Liverpool in the League Cup Semi-final and ultimately lost after two legs, extra time and penalties. Arnautovic had scored again to earn the club a first win at Anfield in over half a century, but despite this memorable feat, two heavy 3 - 0 defeats in the league followed in the days immediately after that cup exit.

Transfer deadline day in January 2016 saw the arrival of Gianelli Imbula for a club record £18.3 million from Porto, and after a hat trick of wins against clubs in the bottom half of the table, Stoke were briefly seventh in the Premier League after twenty eight games. Imbula also scored his first goal for the club in a 3 - 1 victory at Bournemouth.

In March, Jack Butland was on England duty having been in excellent form and was selected to play against Germany in Berlin. Early in the game he suffered a serious ankle fracture. .This was a huge personal blow for Jack who would miss the Euro 2016 Finals. It was also a major setback for Stoke City. He would appear in just a handful of games for the club during the next twelve months.

Stoke's back up goal keeping options were the ageing Shay Given and Danish keeper, Jakob Haugaard. Neither were adequate replacements for Jack.

Heavy defeats followed at Liverpool, Man City and at home to Spurs (conceding a dozen goals in the process). This characterised the ups and downs of the season. However, Stoke still achieved a ninth place finish for the third year running with a late comeback against West Ham at home on the final day of the season. Imbula scoring the winner in front of the Boothen End.

This was a season when Marco Arnautovic had stamped his authority on the Premier League. He was Stoke's top goal scorer with twelve successful strikes and was involved in almost everything positive that the club achieved.

Following this 2015/16 season, a season of both magically sweet highs and horribly sour lows, our Manager, Mark Hughes was instantly under pressure and scrutiny. Three consecutive ninth place finishes in the most competitive league in the world provided precious little fire cover for Hughes, as we embarked on a new campaign with all the dials set back to zero.

In the close season, the arrival of Joe Allen was greeted positively, as was the signing of Wilfred Bony brought in on loan. If Bony could rediscover the devastating form he displayed at Swansea and then Man City, there was genuine hope that we may have found a twenty goal a season striker.

The 2016/17 pre-season failed to inspire across five away games, though did culminate in a fun trip to Hamburg. Here Stoke fans enjoyed a rare opportunity to watch from a steep terracing area reserved for away fans in the corner of the impressive stadium. The acoustics within the Volksparkstadion were fully exploited (as well as the occasional beverage) and fans remained in the ground long after the final whistle. This proved entertaining for the locals who looked on in disbelief as the full repertoire of anthems rang out loudly and fans cavorted as if they had won a vital cup tie rather than lost 1 - 0 after a sterile display against SV Hamburg.

While the record signing of Imbula was a gamble, he had initially impressed with bustling midfield performances and some crucial goals. Not only was he the record signing by some margin, he also signed a lucrative five and a half year contract. As a clearly talented player (albeit particularly one footed), Stoke had the opportunity to make a profit on Imbula after his initial glimpses of quality had alerted Juventus. Instead the club chose to place him at the centre of its plans rather than sell him at that stage.

However, while in Orlando during pre-season, Imbula fell out with team mates, the management, coaching staff and ultimately the club in irretrievable fashion. He effectively substituted himself towards the end of a friendly match.

After a season of long discontent, appearing on just nine occasions, the player had badly lost his way. Stoke spent the close season in Summer of 2017 trying to find a club to take him off their hands. The discontent appeared to stem partly from the style of play at Stoke. He didn't mix with his playing colleagues, refused to learn the English language and proved a handful to manage.

The gamble on Imbula had not paid off and a series of unremarkable loan deals failed to recoup much of the carrying cost of his salary with all but no chance of any capital likely to ever flow back into the club.

On 22nd February 2020, four long years and three weeks after being signed by Stoke, his contract was finally terminated. He played only twenty six times for the club and scored just twice.

After the *eventful* pre-season, it was important that Stoke started well in their 2016/17 Premier League campaign. The stadium had been expanded, spruced up and looked stunning with the addition of two thousand six hundred additional seats in a previously open corner of the ground. This brought the capacity of the stadium to just over thirty thousand and it was also rebranded the Bet365 stadium as our generous owners continued to heavily invest in the club that they had bankrolled with over £200m.

Unfortunately, they didn't get the desired positive start, as victories eluded the club for over two months. The return from the first seven games was a paltry three points. Scoring goals appeared hard work with only five goals netted in this opening sequence of games. The loan signing of Wilfred Bony failed to ignite our misfiring attack.

Conceding goals came far more naturally however, as our net bulged sixteen times in these games. The televised 4 - 1 defeat at Crystal Palace was shocking and even a stunning late strike by Arnautovic failed to lighten the mood.

Now the pressure was really on.

Veteran Shay Given found life difficult replacing the injured Jack Butland. Fortunately, the signing of Lee Grant proved a positive acquisition between the posts and he enjoyed a good run of first team football, performing strongly (thank goodness).

The season progressed in uninspiring fashion. Gone were the days of victories against the fashionable top six. However, crucial wins were achieved against clubs struggling at the foot of the table and Stoke finished thirteenth with a goal difference of minus fifteen having netted just forty one times. Top scorer was the ageing Peter Crouch with seven successful strikes.

In this seasons January transfer window the Coates family shelled out a further £12 million for Saido Berahino, a long time transfer target from West Brom. While he initially struggled for match fitness, he played eight times without scoring during the remainder of the season.

Berahino had been a proven goal scorer at West Brom. The transfer fee of £12 million was considerably less than Stoke (and other clubs) had previously bid for the striker. The five and a half year contract was however especially generous.

We had played our cards and gambled on an instinctive fifteen to twenty goal a season Premier League striker. The gamble backfired. It took Berahino nineteen months to register his first goal for the club. This was nine hundred and thirteen days since his last goal in professional football. His attitude and behaviour was shocking. He spurned chance after chance to prove his worth and despite the fans backing him loyally, he failed to repay that generous support. In the end there was just nowhere else to go with the wayward player and led to the termination of his contract in August 2019.

The season neared its conclusion with a demoralising 4 - 1 defeat in the final home game against Arsenal where the stadium was almost empty by the time the players performed their customary end of season lap of the pitch.

Even an enjoyable victory in fine weather on the final day of the season at Southampton barely lifted spirits and couldn't paper over the widening cracks. Hughes was under even more pressure now and the divisions in the fan base were becoming ever more visible.

Against this backdrop, the 2017/18 season was always going to be a significant challenge. So it proved.

Stoke were desperate for a positive close season and transfer window. It was widely recognised that goals were in short supply.

Ahead of the new season there were various departures from the club, including strikers Jon Walters and Joselu. Walters was a loyal servant nearing the end of his career and after two hundred and twenty six appearances and forty three goals in seven years at the Club, he left with everyone's good wishes. However Joselu, who appeared and scored four goals in pre-season was also sold to Newcastle. With goal scoring a clear and obvious challenge, this appeared a strange decision.

The worst was yet to come when Marco Arnautovic, together with his brother (also his agent) engineered his transfer to West Ham. While this brought in over £20 million it was a body blow. He had been Stoke's best player in 2015/16 and again in many of the games in the 2016/17 season, chipping in with valuable goals.

Prior to the news that Arnautovic was seeking a move away from the club, six of our fan group had already made arrangements to attend the now customary pre-season game in

Germany. These pre-season excursions had become a fixed part of the itinerary for Dan and I, we loved the trips to both Cologne and Hamburg and were now off to Eastern Germany, joined by Steve and his son Joe as well as Ade and his wife Sallie. RB Leipzig were our opponents.

RB Leipzig were an emerging force in the Bundesliga, founded as recently as 2009, whose sponsors (Red Bull) had generously supported their rise. Their stadium, the Red Bull Arena is impressive with an all seater capacity of almost forty three thousand. They had finished second in the Bundesliga and qualified for the Champions League for the first time. Not bad just eight years after forming!

Together with around a thousand other Stoke fans we descended upon the attractive city of Leipzig where we enjoyed drinks and food in a friendly, sun drenched environment. Supporters congregated in a pedestrianised city centre area with bars and restaurants lining both sides of a narrow street. We enjoyed several hours before and after the match taking in the sun and atmosphere.

There was a healthy crowd of some twenty thousand in the ground and Stoke's away following made themselves heard throughout the game, despite falling behind early on to a penalty. Just before half time Diouf glanced in a corner from Shaqiri to equalize.

The winner fell to Stoke as another cross from Shaqiri caused confusion in the home defence and a Leipzig defender looped a header over his own keeper. Cause for a fulsome celebration in the stands.

These pre-season trips often provided some of the more memorable highlights of the season, which is how it proved to be in 2017/18.

Ahead of the start of the new Premier League season, and with limited striking options remaining, the club was naturally keen to add fire power to the squad. Two strikers joined the club, Jese on loan from PSG and Eric Maxim Choupo-Moting. Neither of these players proved to be the answer to our goal scoring problems nor were they adequate replacements for Arnautovic. Between them in their combined thirty four appearances they delivered six goals.

The defence was strengthened with the signings of centre halfs Bruno Martins Indi from Porto and Kurt Zooma on loan from Chelsea. One last signing was also made when yet another centre half, Kevin Wimmer joined the club for an astonishing £18 million. This was an inexplicable piece of recruitment which was to result in an even worse outcome than the Imbula debacle.

Wimmer's move raised eyebrows. Spurs had paid Cologne £4.3 million for him in 2015. Two years and only thirteen Premier League starts later and his value had more than quadrupled. He was part of a Stoke defence that conceded fifty goals in the first twenty three games of the season. The half-century being racked up in a 3 - 0 defeat at Old Trafford.

Wimmer hasn't played for Stoke since. He has been out on loan in Germany at Hannover and onto Belgium with Royal Mouscon. He remains under contract until 2022.

A predictably tough season unfolded with our home advantage enabling some vital victories against fellow struggling clubs. At the turn of the year Stoke were in fifteenth place, two points off the bottom three in a congested league table. Goal difference was minus twenty three, comfortably the poorest in the division.

Notably, Stoke City scored three times to beat bottom of the league West Brom at home on 23rd December. Little did we know that we would have to wait almost twenty three months before watching our team score three goals in another game.

The New Year started badly with a 1 - 0 reverse at home to Newcastle, who themselves were struggling and before the game were below Stoke in the league. After their victory the Geordies advanced to thirteenth place while Stoke fell to sixteenth, perilously close to the relegation zone.

The next fixture was the FA Cup 3rd round tie at Coventry City.

By this time, the combination of poor performances on the pitch, a predictable lack of goal threat and ridiculous levels of ill-discipline off the pitch meant that what was a divide between supporters about Hughes position as manager shifted to a unanimous call to dismiss him. It was noticeable that the Board hesitated for a further five matches across December and up to the FA Cup defeat at Coventry in early January before acting to remove Hughes.

If the club's owners were generous, they were also very loyal.

Those of you who read my earlier book, *Glory Hunter*, will know that I have a real issue with Coventry City. Living in Rugby during my childhood, they were the closest Division One football club. For years they dodged relegation from the Division.

In the 1976/77 season, when Stoke City were relegated along with Spurs and Sunderland, Coventry played out a draw against Bristol City which ultimately saved both teams. Jimmy Hill had ordered a delay to kick off due to *crowd congestion* and they played out the final ten minutes like a pre-season friendly as the score of Sunderland's match at Everton was relayed over the tannoy.

In the 1984/85 season Stoke City were again relegated from Division One in a dreadful season for the Club where we accumulated just seventeen points and in the process, a minus sixty seven goal difference. Coventry City were also in peril and needed to win all three of their final games to stay up. In the first of this sequence of games they had beaten Luton and next travelled to North Staffordshire to face Stoke at the Victoria Ground.

Coventry were leading 1 – 0 at Stoke with six minutes remaining when we were awarded a penalty. Ian Painter our top goal scorer during the season with six goals stepped up and crashed his spot kick against the underside of the bar and down. It appeared to be well over the line. The ball bounced away and the goal was not awarded.

Just when you really need goal line technology.

They proceeded to beat Everton, who had already been crowned Champions of Division One, 4 – 1 on the final day of the season to stay up, again.

Coventry City were eventually relegated in 2001 and again in 2012. I'll leave it there, though there is *so* much more.

My dilemma now was that I knew Mark Hughes needed to be dismissed, but could I stomach losing to the Sky Blues from two leagues below, to seal Hughes' fate? The only saving grace was that I was in Sydney watching the final test match of the ashes at the time and as the cup match was kicking off at 2am local time, I decided not to try and find a venue to watch it.

When I awoke, the stream of messages on my mobile told me all I needed to know. We had lost. Hughes was sacked.

Murmurings around the club echoed more discontent and the fan base was divided on whether he should have left the club in the Summer of 2017. In hindsight, this would have been better for all parties. Hughes could have departed with his reputation intact after four solid years in the Premier League and Stoke would have the close season to recruit a new manager in an orderly fashion.

The apparent panic and desperation in the managerial search that followed was not elegant. The club pursued several preferred managerial choices including Gary Rowett, Quique Sanchez Flores and held talks with Martin O'Neill. None of these targets were persuaded to accept the job.

Ultimately, it was Paul Lambert who was appointed on 15th January 2018.

Paul Lambert was an accomplished midfielder who won forty caps for Scotland and was a European Cup winner with Dortmund. He managed seven clubs before Stoke, including Aston Villa in the Premier League. I don't know a single person who thinks he is a dislike-able bloke. But neither is he an entirely inspiring (fourth choice) appointment and as a communicator can be difficult to understand - he appears to mumble a lot.

It wasn't long before the experienced Lambert became exasperated by the lack of professionalism within the Stoke squad. A rigorous fines system was imposed to restore discipline. Wimmer and Berahino were placed on special fitness programmes.

Paul Lambert won in his first game in charge at home to Huddersfield, fuelling hopes of a revival. It was the *only* game he won prior to relegation being confirmed.

Lambert was quick to identify Shaqiri as Stoke's best chance of beating the drop. He was the remaining class act in the squad and did manage eight goals and seven assists during the season. It was a season in which Shaqiri contributed 13% of our goals scored and a staggering 25% of expected assists.

In our next sequence of fixtures, he scored the opener at Bournemouth before we eventually lost the game 2 – 1. The following week he scored the equaliser in the home game against Brighton, before we missed an injury time penalty to seal all three points and in our next match at Leicester scored again to give us a one goal lead at half time, before Jack Butland conceded a clumsy own goal in the second half to deny us the points.

Another of his individual moments of brilliance gave Stoke hope in their penultimate game of the season as we took a crucial lead against Crystal Palace. However, this was also overturned by two second-half Palace goals which condemned Stoke City to defeat and the end of a decade in the Premier League.

In the meantime, Mark Hughes had moved on to become Southampton manager who were also struggling. They stayed up, just, (I hesitate to say that *he* kept them up) on the last game of the season. He would soon get his just deserts in the following season when he was duly sacked, again. He lasted less than nine months (which included the close season).

Many felt sorry for Paul Lambert, who inherited a near impossible situation. I don't doubt he was decent man who tried hard (and had some moments of bad luck) but the statistics tell the full story. These confirm that he won only two of his fifteen league games in charge - the first and the last. The last was a dead rubber at Swansea and without Jack Butland's heroics in goal in that game, he wouldn't have won that one.

Lambert's tenure was ended within a week of our final game. It can't have been a big surprise to him.

It was now time to rebuild at Stoke, and by God we needed some heavy machinery to do that.

CHAPTER THREE

Reflections on the catastrophe

A large part of the problem over several years has been recruitment at Stoke City. Some of the events were beyond the club's control. For example, the exits of Nzonzi and Arnautovic. Though in Nzonzi's case the £7 million we received didn't represent his full market value.

As for Arnautovic, he became a target of fans, seemingly just leaving for more money to a club of similar status and size at the time. However, many have now come to recognise that for him, at his peak, it was not unfair for him to seek the next step on the ladder and a considerable uplift in remuneration.

I (now) prefer to remember the class and skill he displayed for Stoke City on the pitch. He arrived as *damaged goods* and left, after rehabilitation and given an opportunity at Stoke, a world class player.

When truly class players depart, there is inevitably a deep void. The key objective and action is the replacement strategy. Neither Nzonzi or Arnautovic were adequately replaced (despite the willingness of our generous owners to support new player acquisitions).

The recruitment of Imbula, Berahino and Wimmer is, in hindsight, criminal for a club of our size. Imbula was clearly a talented player, but £18.3 million seemed a massively inflated value. Berahino, also talented, threw away chance after chance. Both signings were relatively understandable - in concept and principle.

Wimmer is the one that is much harder to understand. The extent to which Stoke undertook their due diligence on Wimmer is debatable. He rarely played for Spurs. If we even needed another centre half rather than a proven goal scorer, how did he ever command such a value? It appears one of the worst transfers in the history of our club, now the oldest in the entire football league.

Activity in the transfer market is, by its nature, a calculated gamble. The Executive Management of the club have some very positive examples to point to. Arnautovic for example was signed for £2 million and ultimately sold for £20 million plus. Jack Butland was signed from Birmingham for £3.3 million and, having appeared as No 1 for England was valued at hugely more than that (prior to his eventual transfer to Crystal Palace at a lower fee in October 2020). Nzonzi cost £3 million and sold for £7 million etc.

However, the combination of the three disastrous signings above for c£50 million created the chasm into which the club effectively fell into. Some clubs have gotten away with these types of gamble. Some, like Stoke, have not.

It's a sad story with six crucial events that, together, proved too much for our club to sustain, while playing in the most competitive league in the world.

Perhaps if we had managed two or three of the situations in a stronger and more successful manner, we would be in a different place today. However, the truth is that the decline of the club hadn't ended when we were relegated from the Premier League.

But that's another chapter.

CHAPTER FOUR

Swansea Away

As we get in our car it's 7.45am on Saturday 12th May 2018 and Stoke City's final match of the season. It's also the end of our ten year spell in the Premier League.

It's a long way, one hundred and eighty two miles from our home in Northampton. We will be supporting our team already mathematically relegated, at the furthest away ground in the league for us.

It wasn't certain who would play in this final episode of the series. We might have played a second team and got hammered. As it happens, we fielded as strong a side as we could put out with the addition of Lasse Sorenson, our young Danish midfielder joining the starting eleven. Sorenson became the youngest player to *ever* start a match for Stoke City at eighteen years, two hundred and four days old.

Swansea were also mathematically relegated (or as good as). Their only hope was for an unlikely ten goal swing across their match against us, (which they had to win) and in the game between Southampton and Man City at St Mary's.

All in all, it's a game without any particular pressure. Oh, and it will probably pour down (despite the fair weather forecast). It's South Wales after all.

We planned this trip a month ago when we hoped and prayed it would be an emotional climax to the season, where a win might keep us up to enjoy one more season (at least) in the Premier League. To lessen the blow and break up the trip we have a night out and overnight stay booked in Cardiff, home of the magnificent Principality Stadium, just a stone's throw from the city centre. So, the agenda comprises a few beers and a good meal, followed by a few more beers and the inevitable constant banter about Stoke City.

We reminisce; remember the good times. The battling side during the Macari era, with tough uncompromising centre halfs, Vince Overson, Ian Cranson and Noel Blake. The local derby victories against the Vale are always mentioned. The magic of Mark Stein's goals and his winner at Wembley when we lifted the Autoglass Trophy in 1992.

Promotion seasons, and notably those of 1979 back to Division One, courtesy of a magical last minute diving header by Paul Richardson at Notts County, and of course in 2008 when we sealed our place in the Premier League for the first time.

At the time of the Notts County game, I was eighteen years old living in Rugby and travelled to Stoke games by any means I could, by train, coach on my motorbike and most commonly with friends who owned cars who I persuaded to take me to matches. It was before I met the fan group I am now a member of and have attended games with for over thirty years.

Unbeknown to me at the time, all my current mates were also on the pitch after our famous, dramatic late goal clinched promotion at Meadow Lane. Among ten thousand Stoke City fans we all celebrated.

In 2008 it was different, we were all together with the addition of sons and daughters and were again on the pitch at the end of the match to celebrate our promotion, this time at the Britannia Stadium.

Our reminiscing includes classic away trips to Brighton for a relegation party on the beach after a 4 - 1 win. To Anfield in the League Cup where we snatched a 2 - 2 draw when Tony Kelly raced clear before nutmegging Bruce Grobbelaar to equalise for the second time, right in front of eight thousand delirious travelling fans.

Last minute winners such as in our home debut in the Premier League against Aston Villa is a popular and enduring memory, where Mamady Sidibe glanced in a Rory Delap trademark long throw in injury time to win the game 3 - 2.

And always, the crushing of Liverpool 6 - 1 to inflict their heaviest ever defeat in the Premier League.

We talk formations, best goalkeeping moments, best striker ever and worst players to pull a Stoke shirt on. The subject matter is endless and to us, its enthralling.

Dan and I headed off earlier than necessary to Cardiff, diverting to Taunton where Somerset (my county of birth) were playing Hampshire in the County Championship, so a relaxing day's cricket in the sun preceded our adventure across the Severn Bridge.

Crossing the Severn Bridge, the entrance to South Wales, was spectacular on this occasion and we were welcomed with bright sunshine. I was prepared with a pocket full of change to shell out the usual £5.60 on the Toll fee and was pleasantly surprised to be reminded that it's now Toll free. *Whooey*, that's two free pints of Brains then! Parking up adjacent to the Principality Stadium brought back fond memories of almost sixteen years to the day when we comfortably defeated Brentford 2 - 0 in the League One play-off final to regain our place in the Championship.

Strange isn't it that the euphoria of that day contrasts sharply with the misery associated with this year's relegation as we, once again, earned our place in the Championship. Of course, the circumstances are very different, we have enjoyed a decade in the sunshine of the Premier League, have a much stronger squad (on paper) and are financially very secure.

When we visited in 2002, we had Icelandic owners who certainly played their part, bringing in a number of Icelandic players and Manager, Gudjon Thordarson.

On that brilliantly sunny day, 11th May 2002, Stoke City were set to earn a return to the Championship from League One backed by almost forty thousand colourful, noisy fans at the Millennium Stadium, now renamed the Principality Stadium. It didn't all go entirely to plan however. We had drawn the South changing room.

In the three years since the magnificent stadium was christened, the eleven football teams and three rugby teams who had occupied these Southern facilities had all lost. This sequence of events was around an 8,000/1 shot.

Stoke were easily the better team on that day and were superior all over the pitch. We also needed a bit of special help. This came in the form of Andrew Vicari, European Artist of The Year 1995, who was brought in by feng shui expert Paul Darby. Darby had previously been engaged to help lift the changing room curse at the stadium and had led a horse around the pitch, rang a Tibetan bell and sprinkled incense on the pitch.

This was to no avail as subsequent occupants of the Southern changing room facilities also proceeded to lose. First Cambridge United in the LDV Trophy final and then Chelsea, losing in the FA Cup Final to Arsenal, as the jinx continued to claim more victims.

Ahead of our play-off final at the stadium, Vicari painted a seven foot high blazing suns mural in the South dressing room in a further attempt to break the jinx. The painting was bright and bold in red, orange and yellow, featuring the rising sun, a galloping horse and a soaring Phoenix.

It worked. We won and the spell was broken. Vicari was also reputedly mistaken for Gudjon Thordarson at the ground on the day of the final.

Of course, Stoke City being Stoke City, Thordarson left his post within a week of that momentous victory after falling out with his fellow Icelandic owners. Not exactly the news that Stoke fans wanted, throwing us into turmoil ahead of a tough first season back in the Championship.

Returning to our current visit to the welsh Capital, our group of six, had all arrived safely in Cardiff ahead of the match in Swansea the following day. We soon got to grips with what the city has to offer, heading first to the Hopbunker, a brilliant basement bar with dozens of real ales and ciders. Here, the predictable debate began - and continued until well after the witching hour, covering all the topics referred to earlier, and more.

The following morning, we enjoyed a hearty Welsh breakfast.

The extent of the night before is often revealed by some of the breakfast choices, in my case the inclination to choose two large slices of black pudding (alongside the usual other fried items). It must be my bodies way of telling me I need to replenish.

I remember being in a Little Chef several years earlier enjoying an Early Riser breakfast (no hangover on this occasion and therefore no requirement for black pudding) when a mother was hastily ordering coffee and breakfast with her two young children. The eldest child of around seven years was asking question after question and you could clearly sense the frustration of mum who just needed that caffeine burst. The child's final question was, "Mum, what's black pudding". Mum didn't answer and inevitably the child repeated the question, over and over again.

Mum eventually snapped and without shouting, put her menu down, leaned toward her son and after a short pause, said just three words. "Dried pigs blood". Then calmly picked up her menu again and chose her food. It was like a scene from the *Matrix* when everything around just froze for a moment, before normal service was resumed.

I had chosen a discreet Stoke City polo shirt to wear as I wasn't sure if it was going to be a full colours day. This was partly due to our embarrassment of being relegated and also partly due to never being quite sure of what kind of reception you are going to receive from the locals. I was remembering our promotion season from League One in 1993 when we visited Swansea at the old Vetchfield ground for a midweek match.

On that occasion, there was a large away following for the midweek evening fixture and all was calm before the game kicked off. The atmosphere changed almost immediately the game was underway and took on the character of a Wales v England encounter.

Swansea took the lead through a well struck volley from Andy Legg that left our on-loan goalkeeper, Grobbelaar, stranded as the ball ended up in the top corner. Losing 1 - 0 at half time, we turned the match around, first with a close range effort from Steve Foley and then, very late on Nigel Gleghorn arrowed a fabulous header into the very top corner to win the game, amid wild celebrations in the away end.

In the large home terrace on the left hand side of the ground there was major unrest as police battled to keep home fans off the pitch. Outside at full time it was carnage as missiles entered the walled, gated area where the away fans were detained. A number of Swansea locals were even trying to scale the walls and fences in an attempt to gain access.

After over half an hour we were able to make our way back to the car which we did, silently.

I needn't have had any concerns this time around as we would be warmly welcomed in Swansea by kindred spirits both suffering the same fate of relegation.

My initial choice of shirt was immediately adjusted after seeing the others with some great, if fluorescent, retro shirt choices. I had also brought my old Cristal Tiles top which bears the 1989/90 badge, one of my favourites, so this was adorned as we headed to the cars. It was a strange day as Cardiff City were going to be parading in the streets later on that day to celebrate their promotion from the Championship, while we of course were already confirmed as passing them in the opposite direction.

Yes, Neil Warnock had done it again, with the Bluebirds this time and was heading back to the Premier League. He was no doubt already preparing for an immediate return to the Championship and most likely the sack mid-way through the season after a string of hopeless performances, leaving the team in the bottom three.

I am not a huge fan of Neil Warnock, but I do like the anagram of his name, *Colin Wanker*. Most of the lads speak very positively about Colin, (I mean Neil Warnock). I remember him most as manager of Sheffield United and as an arrogant, nasty, rude bloke who will only ever be Colin Wanker to me.

The thought of this cheers me up and I always imagined passing him in a corridor and saying, "Hi Colin". What I wouldn't need to do however was imagine his inevitable reaction. I spoke to one of the lads, T4, about this and he confirmed my thoughts saying, "He would either twat you without thinking or with head down *(in his Grinch like pose)* tell you to fuck off".

Enroute to Swansea, Ade and his son, Max were in the advance party tasked with locating a good pub close to the ground with parking. Preferably on the right side of the stadium to enable a good exit from Swansea in preparation for the one hundred and eighty mile return trip home. The lads did a very good job. The pub, The Coopers Arms couldn't have been friendlier as many Swansea fans greeted us in the sunshine, shook hands and shared a beer. They were devastated, not just with the plight of their own club, but in the knowledge that Cardiff City (fierce South Wales rivals) had been promoted.

And we thought we were hard done by.

We entered the ground and after one final Premier League beer, we took our places. We occupied a much larger section of the away end than is normally allocated. More than three thousand Stoke fans filed in adding red and white colour to the Swansea City black and white theme in the ground. The sun continued to shine and the scene was glorious. Deserving of much more than a dead rubber between two already relegated sides.

Occasionally the banter between fans from South Wales and any English team can be a bit tense, often with a nationalistic theme. Such as during that midweek game in 1993. It was nothing like that on this day as fans shared songs about their joint predicament.

The game began briskly with the Swans taking the initiative. But for a superb display by Jack Butland we could have been two or three behind in the opening ten minutes. However, our sieve like defence was pierced after fourteen minutes after a neat but predictable move resulted in a tap in for Andy King to put the home side 1 - 0 up. At this point Stoke fans joined in the singing of "going down, going down, going down" and even sang on behalf of the Swans to score the many goals that might save them.

The reason for this wasn't any particular sympathy with Swansea's position. It was aimed at Southampton and their recently appointed manager, Mark Hughes. Hughes was seen by a large number of Stoke fans as culpable for the club's decline. Southampton were the only team whom Swansea could leap frog to safety if they could achieve the unlikely multiple goal feat.

Before long it was all academic as on an attack of our own, Badou Ndiaye lobbed the keeper to make it 1 - 1. The celebrations were good, but perhaps not as fulsome as in a more meaningful match. It wasn't long before we took the lead with a slick move and assist by Lasse Sorenson. Crouch did the necessary with a trademark header and the celebrations which followed were a bit more like it. It was Crouchy's fifty third and *final* headed goal in his Premier League career.

Swansea's relegation was sealed as Man City were also drawing a blank at Southampton at half time. That match finished 1 – 0 to the visitors.

The second half was a more sterile affair and it felt as if the brutal reality was dawning on the players of both sides. Mid way through the second half, the ball was again crossed toward Peter Crouch where it was intercepted by a Swansea player's hand. Penalty.

This was the final opportunity for Xherdan Shaqiri to get on the scoresheet in Stoke City colours as it was as obvious as the day was long that he would be leaving the club. He took a strange, long run up and almost danced toward the ball. He had scored a perfect penalty at Anfield in the shootout so this shouldn't have been in any way intimidating. In front of him, behind the goal three thousand Stoke fans waited in anticipation.

It was a poor penalty more comfortably saved than any I had seen all season. Typical. I suppose at least he got it on target as in the same fixture almost exactly a year earlier, Arnautovic had a penalty at the same end which he proceeded to blast high over the bar and into the crowd. Penalties were becoming a real issue for us when they should be glorious gifts.

The game was ebbing toward its conclusion and the signal for the away fans to commence a medley of our favourite songs over our Premier League era. The songs came thick and fast, "Ricardo Fuller City's Number 10....."; "Robert Huth, Huth, Huth he's a massive German youth.....", "Kenwyne is a Stokie he comes from Trinidad....." etc, it was a cacophony of noise.

The vocal tribute culminated in an extended passionate version of club favourite of forty years, "We'll be with you" never more poignant than on this occasion and naturally a deafening rendition of "Delilah", which isn't usually appreciated by Welsh fans but which today saw many Swansea fans join in the chorus.

This was a fitting send off after a decade in the Premier League, an FA Cup Semi and Final at Wembley and a valiant Europa League campaign.

As well as enthusiastically participating, I was staggered by the volume created by our largest following to South Wales since the play-off final of 2002.

This really meant something to the fans and it made our long journey thoroughly worthwhile, eclipsing the fact that we had also won away for the first time since late October when we triumphed 1 - 0 at Watford.

After the final whistle the players congregated by the away fans where some special choruses of "Delilah" and "We'll be with you" were repeated and appreciated by one and all. Our manager, Paul Lambert stood motionless in respect of this tribute as well as a number of the players applauding the fans vigorously.

All the players, even those we knew would depart seemed moved. It was emotional.

I felt in that moment that we had a platform for the future.

CHAPTER FIVE

No one writes about relegation

Relegation is shit.

If a physiatrist were to show me a set of images in a padded room and one appeared with Stoke City under the red line in a football league table, my one word response would be "shit".

No one writes about relegation. All the books and stories are about valiant Cup runs and promotion. Even in mine, *Glory Hunter*, published in the close season in Summer 2017 was filled with more pages about *against the odds* triumphs and *plucky* cup runs. The three relegations that occurred in 1977 and 1985 (from Division One to Division Two), and in 1990 (from Division Two to Division Three) are reported, but naturally not with the same passion and enthusiasm.

Being relegated is a punishing experience. It's a long, slow death punctuated with shit. In the Premier League, it's thirty eight games long and though occasionally you are put out of your misery with a few games to go, it's still torture.

Some football fans (and this one in particular) harbour irrational thoughts and hope of being able to avoid relegation. This is despite a string of the poorest performances, lack of goals and goal threat and a defence leaking goals like a sieve. Even when the writing is on the wall in indelible ink this unrealistic hope can't be fully extinguished. Sometimes it's the hope that causes the most pain.

As long as a slight chance exists, a faint glimmer of hope or chance of recovery the alter ego holds on to the mathematical possibility of salvation. Despite the overwhelming odds.

Then it happens. Your team wins a game out of the blue, often against a far stronger side, well away from any relegation worries. Those three points are food and drink to the eternal optimist alter ego, feeding on scraps and waiting to remind you that it's not over. Now, maybe if we can win two or three games in a row and the others around us lose a few, we can still escape.

It's all bollocks of course as back to back wins in the Premier League are rare. And as you observe the teams around the relegation places keeping you company *achieve* that unusual feat, the dreadful realisation that there is no escape returns like a tidal wave.

It's with around ten games remaining that you perform a senseless detailed project to predict the results of all the games left. This isn't just for your team, oh no. It includes all the others who are in it up to their necks or who might get dragged into trouble. This is a major feat. It requires objectivity and honesty to produce a set of predicted results for all the relegation contenders that looks and feels like a genuinely possible outturn.

The result is an algorithm that's more complicated than the Governments model for moderating and determining exam results for GCSE and A Level students during the Covid-19 Pandemic. It's also about as much use.

It's complete bollocks.

The guiding principle and etiquette is that when you share the work with your similarly suffering fan mates, they would nod their heads and accept it as a reasonable assessment. It never is, because they are like you. They want to believe the possibility of revival and escape even though they know it's futile.

The prediction outturn breathes life into the now almost dormant optimist alter ego. It confirms that three wins from those remaining ten games will be achieved (even though this ratio of victories hasn't been achieved over the previous twenty eight games of the campaign). The prediction is that enough points will be secured and relegation will be avoided - *just*.

The best bits are the predictions also made for the other six or eight clubs in a similar predicament. You convince yourself that you are being honest about what they will achieve. This usually means forecasting draws between teams in trouble when they play one another and losses against the invincible top six. At least applying this rule is fair, it's just, and for your team it's correct.

The problem is that for some of the others in trouble, it's not correct. For example, Swansea beat Liverpool and Arsenal in consecutive games (both invincible teams in the top six where defeats were obvious and forecast), West Ham beat Chelsea and Brighton also beat the badly wilting Arsenal.

But that's ok, we play Arsenal soon too and a chance for us to out-perform the predicted loss and nil points, taking advantage of their plight. This is also bollocks.

In our ten years of Premier League football, we haven't taken a single point from the Emirates - unlike every other *invincible* team. We had won at Man City through that amazing Diouf solo effort. We managed the feat at Spurs (twice), with Whelan crashing in a late winner and in a more accomplished performance, Bojan and Walters doing the damage. We drew twice at Liverpool and managed a draw at both Man Utd and Chelsea.

But never one solitary point at Arsenal.

Luckily, Arsenal continue a terrible and embarrassing run of games and results until the end of March. Our match against the Gunners was on April 1st. It's televised and the performance they deliver sees a transformed side. Playing like a combination of Man City, Real Madrid and Barcelona. We lose 3 - 0.

Alter ego optimist is a bit quiet, but not for long. He pipes up with "well, we expected this in the prediction forecast so it's no big deal. We have home games to follow against lesser sides where we will deliver the performances, get the results and secure the points to save our season".

Surely it's time to face the truth. We're fucked and we know we are. But no, lets stumble and claw our way through the next passage of games, hoping that we can arrive at the final game of the season, away at Swansea, where a win and three vital points will keep us up.

We know however that this scenario is very unlikely. Even if we did, by some miracle, find ourselves in this luxurious position, we would still manage to screw things up on that last day, most likely against a team with nothing to play for with a group of players mentally already in speedos and thinking of Caribbean palm trees, rum cocktails and warm clear seas.

That's why no one writes about relegation.

It's depressing.

It's shit.

CHAPTER SIX

Back in the Championship

The Championship. A grand name for the league which disguises the fact that it's actually Division Two.

You can view this league in three ways.

First and most optimistically, the gateway to the Premier League. True of course, but like the contestants in "It's a Knockout" wearing oversized costumes and heading for a narrow channel through which just one would pass, it's usually carnage. Three teams do escape the Championship through the sky light, the first two by right and the third through a play-off contested by the four next best teams in the league.

The escape to the Premier League feels good and is vigorously celebrated, but before the hangover subsides, the reality of the prospect of probably the hardest season to ever come hits hard. This is reinforced when Bet365 and Paddy Power make your team odds on for a swift return to the Championship, before a ball has even been kicked.

The second way of viewing the Championship, and worst of all, is the prospect of another relegation, this time to League One. League One sounds quite regal, like its top of the pack. It's actually Division Three, the second lowest professional football league in England.

It is easy to underestimate the Championship, something often done by Premier League teams who have been recently relegated. It's a forty six match grind, a marathon which means loads of midweek fixtures as well as the usual weekend games - and that's before any League and FA Cup games on top of that.

So, the prize ponies of the Premier League, who somehow find themselves in the Championship have a serious adjustment to make. Gone are the days of just thirty eight games played in almost entirely full and impressive stadia across England and, in occasional seasons, South Wales.

Sunderland, who were relegated from the Premier League in 2017 found themselves in this position and ultimately dropped out of the Championship after their first season back in the second tier. They have failed to make a rapid return.

The third view of the Championship and most common, is the section of the division occupied by the majority of clubs in the league. They occupy the mid table of the Championship. Most have previously been in the Premier League and boast proud histories. They harbour thoughts of a push toward promotion but probably fear the likelihood of relegation even more. It's incredibly competitive.

All in all, it's a very tough division indeed and this is exacerbated for Stoke City by the number of Midlands derbies which increases the local tension and fight for valuable points. With Aston Villa, Birmingham, Derby, Nottingham Forest, West Brom and Stoke City all fighting it out with close Midlands neighbours, it looks and feels like an edition of Division One from the late 1970's and early 1980's.

Other Midlands clubs have also appeared and disappeared. Stoke for a decade in the Premier League, Aston Villa every now and again and previously, Coventry City (I would like to think would never resurface, but even with financial woes and no home stadium, the irritating Sky Blues have only gone and gotten themselves promoted back into the championship for the 2020/21 season).

Leicester have managed to shake off the badge of a Championship Club, cemented by their astonishing Premier League title in 2015/16. Also Wolves, who, in just two seasons in the Premier League look reborn and capable of a long stay.

What we do know about life in the Premier League, is that it's a fragile existence. A poor run of results and the pressure is on, with the Championship waiting, like a hungry predator, or quicksand, ready and waiting to consume those clubs who weaken and fall into the drop zone.

CHAPTER SEVEN

The end for Lambert, the start for Gary Rowett

Gone was Paul Lambert, who failed in his attempt to keep us in the Premier League. A decent man trying to manage an almost unmanageable squad in a desperate situation.

If a few things had gone our way we could easily have stayed up and been able to secure our eleventh season in the top flight. Three specific examples in games stand out.

First, in our twenty seventh league game at home to Brighton and Hove Albion in early February. Just shy of thirty thousand spectators were in the Bet365 stadium, almost a capacity crowd to urge Stoke toward a crucial victory and three points against fellow strugglers. Brighton led at half time by a single goal until Shaqiri scored to level after sixty eight minutes.

With time ticking away, and the full ninety minutes played, Stoke are awarded a fairly soft penalty for a challenge on Jese. Charlie Adam seizes the ball in readiness to take the penalty. Jese goes *bananas* as he wants to take the spot kick. His antics were truly juvenile and as his protests continued, he really did make himself look a complete idiot.

We will never entirely know how much these actions and the delay that ensued affected Charlie who was still holding the ball and waiting for the moment that the penalty could be taken. Eventually the ball is on the spot and Charlie steps up. It's a fairly ordinary connection and a poorly placed penalty which the keeper is able to save. The ball bobbles free just yards from an empty goal with the keeper helpless on the floor.

Charlie, in almost frozen slow motion should reach the ball first and tap it in. It's excruciating. He gets there at the same time as a defender diving in from just behind to challenge. The ball goes for a corner and the challenge (far more of a penalty than the first offence) is ignored by the referee.

Two points dropped.

Second, away at Leicester City on 24th February, in the game following the Brighton fiasco. Shaqiri (who else) had given us the lead again with a well struck and directed shot from outside the box (like all his goals really). The ball beat Schmeichel all ends up and gave us a 1 - 0 lead to take into the half time interval.

It was always going to be a challenge to hold out with a single goal advantage at Leicester. They are a good side and would be throwing the kitchen sink at us in the second half. The reality was actually much calmer than that. Leicester were certainly on top but we were holding them off fairly successfully.

That was until they broke down the right and from a tight angle the ball was crossed, waist high, far too close to the keeper. We fully expected Jack Butland to gather the ball. Instead, Butland's positioning was at fault and he juggled the ball into the net for an own goal. We saw the rest of the game out without any particular drama.

Two more points dropped.

Third, away to West Ham on 16th April. With games running out and things becoming increasingly desperate, there was a strong turnout of Stoke fans for this crucial night match at the soulless London Stadium. In what was a tight, hard fought game, the Hammers still had three efforts ruled out for offside. Two of these were fairly obvious decisions. We held our breath the third time as the crowd seemed very interested in the attempt, but fortunately the linesman had flagged.

As the game drew on and into its final fifteen minutes, we were pressing for the goal that would earn the precious three points. From the edge of the West Ham box at the away fans end of the ground, Shaqiri twisted, turned and got a low shot away. Joe Hart dived down to save and fumbled what should have been a regulation save into the path of Peter Crouch.

Crouchy wasted no time in dispatching the loose ball, scoring from close range on seventy nine minutes and approached the away fans who by this time were a bundle of limbs in an ecstatic celebration.

Was this the moment we would finally turn the corner and give ourselves a chance of escaping from the bottom three in the league?

With ninety minutes played, all eyes were on the referee who had signalled four minutes of added time. Well into that period, the ball was crossed toward Andy Carroll. He swung at the ball with an awkward looking volley. Of course, it went in and we were denied again. This felt like the final nail in the coffin.

A further two points dropped, in the most painful circumstances.

I remained with my son in the away end staring at the pitch, the last to leave the ground ushered out by stewards and knowing that our chance had come and gone. Always hoping for the best, but now also planning for the worst.

Just being able to close out two of these three games would have saved us. However, the truth is that would not have been pretty. We were a shambles and would have suffered under the knife of infinitely superior opposition, or even just more organised, ordinary opposition. There would be little that the wealth of our generous local owners, the Coates family, could do about it.

As I described in the chapter about our final game of the season at Swansea, I and many fans felt that we could return to the Premier League at the first time of asking, hopefully with a stronger spirit and with a nucleus of key players remaining at the club. We knew some would depart, Shaqiri for instance, albeit at a transfer price only marginally above what we paid to reflect a release clause in his contract (without which he would not have joined our club in the first place). Liverpool benefited from this and snapped him up like a bargain on the first day of New Year sales.

It rapidly became clear that Stoke's board were wholly committed to a swift return to the Premier League. The target was to do this at the very first attempt. While Stoke continued to invest heavily, the likes of Swansea, also relegated at the same time took a different approach. They sold players and cut costs, and accepted their fate and the need to start again.

Stoke moved to appoint Gary Rowett as manager in June, an initial target when Mark Hughes was put out of his misery. He possessed experience and solid knowledge of the Championship, having managed both Birmingham City and Derby County in the same league. The fans understood this logic, and while he wasn't an immediately likeable character (very little *grip and grin* from this man) there was belief that he could steer us back to the promised land.

If the fans needed any further persuading, it came in the form of the transfer kitty that was made available. More than £40 million was spent on players in his first transfer window. Fans of some Championship clubs accused Stoke of *buying* the league after the signings of Benik Afobe from Wolves for £12 million (payable in January), Tom Ince from Huddersfield for £10 million, Peter Etebo, Nigerian International for £6 million, Sam Clucas from Swansea for £6 million and James McClean from West Brom for £5 million.

Many fans, myself included wanted to believe it so much we were swept along with the hype. All the time underestimating the challenge of the Championship.

Stoke were immediately installed as promotion favourites by the bookmakers. The odds of Stoke being promoted back to the Premier League at the first attempt were as narrow as 7/4 and just 11/2 to be crowned champions. Was there an air of overconfidence and complacency? If so, it changed rapidly once things got underway.

Before that, we were off to Germany again for the usual pre-season jamboree. This time we returned to Hamburg for a match against FC St Pauli, who were in Bundesliga Division Two.

Stoke and St Pauli had formed a partnership in July 2017 and in the first friendly between the clubs in early August 2017, Stoke fans were welcomed to the Millerntor Stadion with free beer at the ground!

On this occasion, a glorious sunny day beckoned fans to a splendid fan park area where beer and optimism were in good supply. Dan and I bumped into Martin O'Shea and his daughter Alice in the open air bar at the ground. They had travelled from Manchester and we were all feeling pretty upbeat. The match itself didn't reinforce the positivity as we lost 2 - 0 to second half goals in front of fifteen thousand spectators. The partnership with St Pauli ended in October 2019.

Now for the real test for Stoke City, their first game back in the Championship away at Leeds United.

CHAPTER EIGHT

Gary Rowett Era - Part One

Month One

With the Championship starting a week before the Premier League, Sky had a fairly obvious choice of fixture as we were drawn away to Leeds United. This was unsurprisingly selected as the prime-time late afternoon game on Sunday 5th August.

It had been hot in Hamburg for the friendly game and only surpassed by an even hotter weekend to welcome in the new championship season, even in Leeds temperatures soared and the crowd swelled to an impressive thirty four thousand.

I had travelled with my two sons, Dan and Tom for this game and we were staying overnight in the City, the plan being a few drinks and a celebratory meal to congratulate ourselves on an opening day win.

It didn't work out that way. Despite being backed by a noisy and fulsome away following who matched the very upbeat Leeds fans inside Elland Road before kick-off. The confidence and expectation of the away support was soon extinguished as Leeds raced into a 2 - 0 lead and nervousness flooded through the side. Even Jack Butland, England's goalkeeper looked out of sorts. New signing Tom Ince had hit the bar from long range in the first half but that was about all there was to cheer.

Half time, 2 - 0 down and in need of a fast start to the second period. Not long into the second half we won a soft penalty and up stepped a new signing to take the spot kick, a striker this time to banish our inadequate goal scoring record. Benik Afobe approached the ball and we stood in huge anticipation.

Our view from the away seats on the side of the ground near the end which we were attacking gave little perspective on the front of the goal. We would only find out if the penalty had been converted by a net bulge. The net did indeed bulge, deeply and we had our goal. More than that, we now had the impetus to step forward and recover the game.

Within two minutes the hope had vanished again as Leeds scored a third goal from a rapid counter attack and very sloppy defending after we had taken a corner.

The game ended in a 3-1 defeat and in reality, we had been well beaten. The chorus in the background was "welcome to the championship" sung vigorously by the Leeds faithful.

I had intended to remove my purple replica away strip at the end of the game in case there was any silliness on the way back into town but it was a hot day, Leeds had won and I couldn't be bothered. I fielded a few predictable comments from some Leeds fans on the way back and in the main it was a sensible walk back into town.

Our dinner still took place, though with less of an upbeat feel attached.

The games come thick and fast in the Championship, though we were not in action in midweek after the Leeds game as we had managed to finish one place off the bottom of the Premier League, due to our victory on the final day at Swansea. This meant it was West Brom who played in round one of the League Cup, (the Carabao Cup), and we could regroup.

Our first home game followed on Saturday 11th August, against Brentford who had been playing really well and who had won convincingly on the opening day.

We're nervous.

An almost full house and another warm sunny afternoon (even in Stoke on Trent) greeted the team. We escaped with a point having taken the lead through a gifted chance gratefully accepted by Afobe after a horrible mix up between the Brentford goalkeeper and defender. We were second best after that and were beginning to realize that life in the Championship was going to be no stroll in the park - we would have to up our game, in every game.

Preston North End away followed. The first scorer in the game was Paul Gallagher. I liked Paul when he played for us a dozen years earlier. Now, however as their talisman, he is really getting on my nerves and any affection is well and truly in the past.

First, he scored from a penalty after a clumsy handball by local boy Tom Edwards. Then, in the second half, he sent an intentional strong forearm into the throat of Joe Allen which pole-axed him. The result of this was not seen by the referee and god forbid that any of the other officials would notice this obvious infringement. He proceeded to be a niggly irritant until he was substituted and was subsequently banned for three games for his violent conduct offence.

The retrospective action taken against players who commit these serious *unseen* infringements means they are correctly suspended. However, this action has no benefit to the teams against whom the infringements were perpetrated. Is it *really* too much to ask that one of the *several* officials at the games are able to witness what's going on and deal with it proportionately? Don't get me started. Linesmen in particular make my blood boil by refusing to make any meaningful decisions without deferring first to the referee, who is often in no position to comment.

As for the game, Erik Pieters smacked in an equaliser with a fabulous half volley, before PNE regained the lead in strange fashion just before the half time interval. Callum Robinson badly sliced an intended shot from the edge of the penalty area which sailed appetisingly to the far post area for Burke to score confidently with a volley. The very large contingent of away fans were less than impressed.

We claimed a draw with a clever back header from Peter Crouch late in the game. Saido Berahino worked hard but drew another blank - we would get very used to that as the season wore on.

Wigan, a newly promoted side, were our next opponents at home. This was surely a good opportunity to claim our first win of the campaign and kick start our season.

Another good crowd were at the Bet365 to back the team. It wasn't long before we knew it not be plain sailing. By half time, we were 2 - 0 down, deservedly. Just ten minutes into the second half it was 3 - 0 and our on loan defender Ashley Williams was sent off after losing his cool and fouling Massey. Boos rang around the ground at full time and Rowett was already making worrying comments such as "....I'll try and turn this thing around".

The stark reality was that we had lost 3 - 0 to a team who had four shots on target and we didn't manage a single one in the entire game. More worryingly, we had failed to win in our last nine home games.

August was drawing to a close soon, and many were glad for that. However, we sparked into life against Hull City the following week and claimed three points after goals from (the less than universally popular) McClean, and an own goal, forced by a Diouf effort were enough to secure a 2 - 0 win.

Midweek saw our final game of August where we dispatched Huddersfield from the Carabao Cup at home, also 2 - 0. It wasn't a classic, but hold the back page, Berahino scored. Just a nine hundred and thirteen day wait for him in professional football!

A bizarre own goal meant a slightly flattering full time score line.

Suddenly we don't want August to end, *ever*.

We drew Nottingham Forest away in the next round of the cup and were keen to resume rivalries with our Midlands neighbours.

Months Two & Three

It's tough love being a Stoke City fan (many fans from many clubs would also say the same). It was already clear that this new league would be a real battle, but it wasn't entirely clear if we were up for it.

One thing that wasn't fully resolved were the necessary adjustments to the squad (both inward as well as outwards) and this would be a longer term project to relieve the club of some legacy signings and unrealistically high wages.

Imbula had departed on loan where at least we recovered some of his wages. There was no sign of any club interested in a permanent deal. Badou Ndiaye and Geoff Cameron also went out on loan. Choupo-Moting joined Paris Saint-Germain on a free transfer. Yes, PSG. But he wasn't good enough for Stoke.

The first game in September was a tough one away at West Brom. The club we had dominated for years during the Pulis era were now getting their own back. To make matters worse our prime Summer transfer target, Dwight Gayle, had elected to go West Brom on loan and promptly scored twice against us. By the time Erik Pieters hit a late thunderbolt to make it 1 - 2, the game was lost.

After the International break Stoke were at Hillsborough. But Dan and I had opted for T20 Finals day at Edgbaston where Somerset were one of the four teams playing out the two semi-finals and then in the evening, the final. I grew up in the Viv Richards, Ian Botham and Joel Garner era and while the current cohort were not at that level, they had looked good in the T20 Blast competition.

I had never attended Finals day before and tickets sell out within weeks of the date being set, which is also before the T20 competition even starts. It was a warm sunny day and Finals day is always a party atmosphere.

We enjoyed a colourful boozy day, only marginally dented because Somerset failed to win their semi against Sussex, and because Stoke threw away a two goal lead at Sheffield Wednesday to draw 2 - 2. Almost all the usual crew were at Hillsborough and it appears we should have been out of sight having convincingly led 2 - 0. However, at least Afobe was getting on the scoresheet and bagged both.

A home win against Swansea followed but then woeful defensive play cost us against Blackburn, also at home, where we conceded three times in the first forty six minutes. We threw everything at them after that and scored twice through Berahino and Tom Ince before being awarded a penalty in the final minute. The penalty was in front of the Boothen End and we prayed for a great escape having been 0 - 3 down.

Berahino was holding the ball and placed it on the spot. He crashed the ball against the crossbar and away to safety. Penalties, as I have mentioned earlier, were becoming a bit of a nightmare for us.

After the emotion of the Blackburn game we were looking forward to a trip to Nottingham where we stayed overnight. This also coincided with Somerset's final Championship Cricket match at Trent Bridge. It was a glorious sunny day, more like the height of Summer than the last morsels of any warm sunshine. The cricket was over quickly as Somerset completed their victory before lunch (with another full day available). A highlight was a hat trick by Craig Overton a tall bustling young fast bowler on the fringe of the England team.

Amazingly it was not the first hat trick of the innings as Somerset skipper Tom Abell achieved the same feat the evening before. An amazingly rare occurrence.

The speed of the victory gave us some extra time in the afternoon and we arrived early at the Brewhouse & Kitchen. This is a good venue, welcoming away fans with views across the river of both Trent Bridge and the City Ground.

The sun was waning as we finished our drinks and headed on the short walk to the ground. I had never seen Stoke win at the City Ground. Three times I had ventured and suffered 5 - 0, 2 - 0 and 1 - 0 losses (which at least were getting narrower).

A good away following were hopeful at kick off and the opening exchanges were even. We conceded after nineteen minutes through a mixture of misfortune and another defensive *Keystone Cops* episode. This was doubled before half time and things deteriorated on fifty minutes as we allowed Lolley time and space to add a third from distance with a low shot.

Hard to believe we would leave the ground in another forty minutes feeling positive about our team and shaking our heads in disbelief that we didn't force extra time.

Having found ourselves three goals behind, Rowett made some subs to freshen it up and it seemed to work. A complacent Forest allowed Afobe to score from close range before panic set in. Now we were totally on top and even Berahino scored after a mix up only a yard from the goal line. At 3 - 2 our chances improved further as clumsy Forest defender Goncalves was dismissed with fifteen minutes to go.

The work rate, effort and commitment were appreciated by the fans and we created a number of half chances and one seriously gilt edged opportunity at the death. Ince sent a perfect cross toward the back post where Berahino was six yards out and unmarked. The ball curved majestically onto the head of our misfiring striker. The keeper was rooted to his position and the goal was gaping.

All that remained was for the header, net bulge and customary celebration. From our angle we saw the ball arrive perfectly, Berahino barely needed to jump. He headed the ball firmly, a good contact. We began to prepare for the goal celebrations when the ball sailed back across goal and somehow beyond the far post.

The celebrations did come, but in the adjacent Forest fans area. They couldn't believe their luck, and we were ruing ours.

Wouldn't it be great when we could play like that final half hour without being 3 - 0 behind?

As well as penalties becoming an issue for us, we were also finding that the feat of scoring three times in a game was elusive.

A few beers on the way back to our hotel finished off a sweet and sour day.

Our final game of the month ended in an entertaining, though uninspiring draw away at the Millers. Rotherham United were adjusting to the Championship after their promotion from League One. Our defensive weaknesses were again on show as again we had to come from 2 - 0 down. And yet again a third goal eluded us.

October brought three wins, a draw and one defeat. A good points haul. However, the reality was different. 1 - 0 away wins at both Norwich and Bristol City were totally against the run of play (at Norwich we won without having a shot on target! An own goal winning the game). We beat a dreadfully weak Bolton 2 - 0 at home and after losing at home to Birmingham, who were backed by a large and boisterous following, we drew at Sheffield United. This was due to a late opportunistic free kick by Joe Allen which crept in low at the goalkeepers near post.

The car journey to Sheffield had been good until the last couple of miles. I had attended Sheffield Hallam University years before as a mature student while studying for an MBA and knew the route to the ground. Steve and Joe were ahead of us, encamped in a pub enjoying a beer. Our attempt to join them was unsuccessful. We eventually did manage to park up on a steep lane adjacent to another pub where we managed to have a slightly rushed pre-match pint.

I especially remember the first ten minutes of the match. It remained 0 - 0 but United carved us apart at will, creating chance after chance. Defensively we looked all over the place and only a combination of poor finishing and great goalkeeping kept us in the game. It was one of those games that every Stoke fan has attended, where the feeling of it's only a matter of *when*, rather than *if* the opposition would score.

It took seventy long, excruciating minutes for the Sheffield United goal, a messy affair which was hard to see from the other end of the ground in the fairly shallow bottom tier of the away end. To recover late on with that free kick was gratefully accepted but my celebrations were muted that night as I felt it papered over some wide cracks.

Nevertheless a good month in terms of points and with seventeen from fourteen games we were seventeenth in the table. Despite our lowly league position, we were now just four points off a play-off place. This was significant as it was the *minimum* expectation of the Board when appointing Rowett and splashing the cash so enthusiastically.

CHAPTER NINE

Gary Rowett Era – Part Two

We were unbeaten throughout November. There were only four games (as there was the obligatory International break) and we drew three and won one. Despite our variable form this lifted us to a lofty twelfth place, five points off a play-off place.

A predictable 0 - 0 draw at home to Tony Pulis's Middlesbrough was followed by another stalemate away at Forest in one of the dullest games I can recall. The only point of controversy was that Afobe, seemingly through on goal was brought down by goalkeeper Pantilimon outside the box. The keeper escaped punishment. On seeing the replay it looked a clumsy challenge on a clumsy striker. James McClean went about reinforcing his relationship with British football fans by refusing to wear a poppy.

We then drew 2 - 2 with QPR after sacrificing the lead late in the second half, and once again the elusive third goal required to win the game didn't arrive. Next up was a midweek home encounter with Derby, whose fans were not at all pleased with Rowett for leaving them to join Stoke. Many Derby fans attended with blow up snakes and made their feelings heard.

That was all the incentive we needed to overcome Frank Lampard's Derby. Derby naturally changed the name of their football club and was now universally known only as *Frank Lampard's* Derby, never as Derby County. He would be gone in less than six months after failing in the play-off Final against Aston Villa. Shame.

Back to the match, Clucas scored the opener with a little help from Frank, no not Lampard, but the keeper Carson this time (who I always refer to as Frank as let's face it, his goalkeeping is comical). We were then reduced to ten men after the sending off of Etebo just after the half hour stage. Our young Nigerian midfielder saw red for a late challenge on Richard Keogh.

This sparked a strange tussle between Joe Allen and Bradley Johnson where Johnson clearly bit Joe solidly and was retrospectively banned for this bizarre incident (again amazing that neither the referee or the other officials saw the offence) and were therefore unable to take the action of sending Johnson off during the game. This retrospective action is all well and good, but as I have already rehearsed, it doesn't benefit the team against whom the offence was committed.

With the score 1 - 0 at half time, my advice to the team is that we need a slow period of nothingness for ten or fifteen minutes to take any sting out of the game. Just ten minutes of sideways passing and then tick the clock down from there.

Five minutes into the second half and Derby were level with a very good free kick by on loan Wilson. We still managed to go on and win the game with Tom Ince scoring against one of his former clubs. Carson was again at fault.

December started away at Reading. We dominated this game and Afobe was guilty of missing several chances in the first half. Despite having to turn around a one goal deficit, we managed to first draw level and then take the lead through a brilliant Ince volley. The injury time equaliser that we conceded was a body blow as we retrenched deeper and deeper in the closing minutes.

We won 2 – 0 the following week at home to bottom club Ipswich Town. Ince was again on the mark and Joe Allen added a second goal. It was enough, without inspiring the home support and for sorry Ipswich and their long and successful history, they were marooned at the bottom of the league with just eleven points from twenty one games and already eight points from safety.

In our next game away at Aston Villa, we were wasteful. We twice took the lead and in general performed strongly (without securing that elusive third goal to seal the match). We had even scored from the spot, Afobe was successful again this time.

We stretched our unbeaten run to ten games in the next match at home to Millwall, Berahino scoring the winner with a header. After this match we were ninth, still just four points off the play offs.

The home game with Millwall on 22nd December marked an unfortunate anniversary. It was the now one full year since we had scored three goals in a football game.

We had been showing some promise, delivered some decent performances and gave the impression we might have a say in this league. But things changed irretrievably in the next three games.

It began with Birmingham away on Boxing Day where we were beaten for the first time in eleven games. Two very well taken strikes sealed our fate at one of Rowett's former clubs. A win would have seen us climb to seventh.

Things became worse in our next game of the festive period away at cash strapped and lowly Bolton. Our last match of 2018 ended 0 - 0 and even though Rowett had installed more organisation and, to a degree stemmed the tide defensively, the games were turgid affairs. The away following displayed their discontent with this showing at the end of the match.

New Year's Day. Always a time for fresh hope and a clean slate. We started brightly at home to Bristol City and earned a penalty early on. Afobe took the kick and sent a woefully weak penalty far too near the keeper who gleefully saved - with considerable ease.

We enjoyed almost 70% possession in the game and still lost 2 - 0. We had seventeen shots with eight on target but scored none. The visitors had two on target and scored with both.

Rowett was clearly feeling the pressure and voiced his displeasure with the fans booing and joining in with songs that opposition fans were singing.

There was no doubt that Rowett's criticism of the fans showing their displeasure increased the tension between him and the supporters. But in the cold light of day, he had won just eight league games in twenty six and there was justifiable criticism about the style of football. He had also reacted angrily to the supporters' calls for Bojan to be restored to the team, pouring fuel on a fire that was already burning brightly.

Emotional and frustrated at the time he made those critical remarks, Rowett would probably reflect now that it was misguided of him to take on the fans.

The Board dismissed him after the 1 - 1 draw in the FA Cup at Shrewsbury. The primary reason for this action was that the team were nowhere near where the board expected them to be. The play-offs were becoming a pipe dream and the Board decided to take a new approach. A *really* new approach.

Reflecting on Rowett's short managerial stint, I don't think it was an abject failure. One or two more converted penalties and a couple less very late goals conceded and we would have been close to where the (*minimum*) Board expectation was.

I think he had the necessary experience, determination and grit. While he wasn't and never tried to be the fans friend, he steadied a club that was infected at branch and root levels. Having to work with the likes of Berahino who, in common with some others took our club for a ride, didn't help him. We had also been wasteful in the final third and while Afobe had scored goals, his conversion rate was poor. Consequently, we never delivered the goals that we required to win enough games.

Rowett's most significant error was taking on the fans. He lost. And his position (almost despite results) became untenable.

Rowett was not out of work long and was soon appointed to become the manager at Millwall where he has instilled the same discipline that he tried to inject at Stoke. Perhaps at that club, who appeared in peril and likely relegation candidates, his methods were enough.

The job of Stoke City Manager has never been an easy one. Rowett joined when the foundations were at their most frail and even the large cash injection wasn't enough to repair the damage. A bit like Covid-19, there is no immediate vaccination, no silver bullet. Recovery will take time.

The challenge facing the club now was preparing for an inevitable second season of gruelling Championship football.

CHAPTER TEN

Beautiful Goals

Long gone were the beautiful goals we occasionally scored in the Premier League. We scored some attractive goals in our first season in the Championship, but they were few and far between.

It's not completely quantifiable what constitutes a beautiful goal.

Is it a scruffy injury time equaliser at St James Park to earn a two all draw, when we had been out of it at 2 - 0 down? The way the ball was gleefully hammered home by centre half, Abdoulaye Faye, returning to his former club and the fans celebration suggested it could well be a beautiful finish.

Perhaps it's a turning and twisting forward, mystifying the Upton Park home defence, beating three men before scoring clinically. City's Number 10 scored many of these beauties.

Is it a slick, quick passing move from your own half ending with a tap in from close range? When Bojan, Arnie and Shaqiri combined at Goodson Park it could easily have been an Arsenal masterclass.

Maybe it's the goal scored from just three touches after leaving the goalkeeper's huge clearance, volleyed in from an almost impossible position from shoulder height into the top corner? We all remember that Crouchy goal against Man City, it was *nearly* as good as Jimmy Greenhoff's effort at St Andrews in 1974, voted ITV's goal of the season. Both were wonderful strikes and beautiful goals.

Sometimes it's the goal you get against that bogey team that leaves the boot like a rocket, sweet as a nut and there's never a doubt where it's going. Cameron Jerome's thunderbolt in the final minute to equalise and make it 3 - 3 at the Brit against Southampton is right up there. My son Tom and I were on the stairs getting ready for a sharp exit on the full time whistle. We enjoyed the celebrations and were happy to be delayed for a while.

Right up there has to be the third goal of an amazing first half performance in our FA Cup semi-final to effectively win the tie. It was executed clinically by our Trinidadian Centre Forward who celebrated with a trademark somersault in front of forty thousand fans in red and white at Wembley.

Or when you're down to ten men early in the first half and keep on battling against Manchester's noisy neighbours. A draw would have been an amazing result let alone a victory. Then, from a perfect Etherington cross and maybe the best header in our Premier League decade we took the lead and defended like lions to preserve a precious and memorable victory. James Beattie was never going to miss out on that chance skilfully presented by Matty. It was a beautiful goal.

Goals at away grounds always stick in the memory, particularly at Chelsea, where we haven't scored many in the last decade. Especially a strike from well inside our own half that flew like a spear over the defence and their six foot four inch tall goalkeeper for a goal of the season candidate. Because it was Charlie we knew it was no fluke, he attempted it in many games.

At White Hart Lane, we witnessed another beauty. This time it was Glenn Whelan's late winner which ignited the fans celebration against Spurs.

Sometimes it's when someone unexpectedly turns up with a goal that generates the most pleasure.

Begovic, our goalkeeper, managed just that from his own penalty box but the one we really wanted was Wilko's goal. He almost achieved it at Wembley in the FA Cup Semi-final when we were 4 - 0 up. Maybe it's best he didn't score then because we all know what's coming if Wilko scores!

Eventually he did score. Just once. A penalty in his own testimonial. It was emotional and he made no mistake. We were on the pitch of course.

Just as emotional was seeing Ricky once more in that testimonial and to watch Steino join the fray brought a tear to my eye. The Golden One. I loved watching him.

More spectacular goals flowed. Steven Nzonzi's sublime curler against Liverpool to put us 5 - 0 up at half time wasn't too shabby. Mame Diouf's amazing run from the edge of our own box away at Man City to nutmeg Joe Hart and steal a 1 - 0 win will never be forgotten.

A few years earlier, Liam Lawrence's long range strike at Hull guaranteed our place in the elite league for a second season. It was a genuine contender.

Maybe eclipsing all these goals was that crazy moment at home, in injury time against Aston Villa, our first home game in the Premier League. We had taken the lead twice, through a Liam Lawrence penalty that was clinically converted and a goal of wizardry by the mercurial Ricardo Fuller, but we had been pegged back on both occasions.

It was a harmless throw in, except no throw in was ever harmless when Rory Delap was involved. The long, flat, missile he was able to project, causing panic in the opposition box. The space was crowded. We had all our big fellas causing a nuisance, among them the understated Mamady Sidibe, a player I once described as not good enough to be leading our front line. Shame on me.

The ball arrived in the sunlight curling slightly as an in-swinger, spinning and with the kind of zip that Shane Warne puts on a cricket ball. The trajectory was the key. Many players can launch a long throw, none have ever been able to arrow the ball with such ferocity and at the angle that Rory did.

His throw into the box in this game was the final roll of the dice, a gamble. A good gamble. It created mayhem (as it did many times before and after). Sidibe's head rose just a fraction above all the straining defenders. He made the slightest of contacts and Villa's keeper, the very able Brad Friedel, was stranded.

As the ball entered the net, the Boothen End went wild, not a single person had left. It was magical. It was the boost we needed, the belief flowed. We welcomed the big boys to our stadium, we bullied them, and quite often defeated them, especially Arsenal and Spurs who crumbled in our theatre, our bear pit.

Maybe that was the most beautiful goal of the era. But I don't care. A scuffed effort that bobbles into the corner from five yards is fine.

Every goal is a thing of beauty, when it's one of ours.

CHAPTER ELEVEN

Enter Mr. Jones

Nathan Jason Jones, was a Welsh professional footballer with almost five hundred appearances. He spent five years at Brighton playing one hundred and fifty nine times and seven years at Yeovil where he played on one hundred and eighty five occasions.

His managerial career, before joining Stoke was a three year stint at Luton Town and a nine day mini spell as caretaker manager at Brighton after Sami Hyypia resigned and before Chris Hughton's appointment on 31st December 2014.

His main achievement at Luton was winning promotion from League Two in 2017/18. He also guided them to a strong position to repeat that feat in the following season. When Jones left Luton for Stoke, they were in second place in League One. This was a position they took advantage of and won promotion back to the championship after a twelve year absence.

Appointing Jones was a significant departure for the Stoke Board. From Pulis to Hughes to Lambert and Rowett the Board valued experience more than anything else. So taking a chance on a man who had managed only one club and never higher than in League One, was a real risk.

The due diligence carried out by the club appeared thorough. An external recruitment agency was commissioned and references and analysis of his development were very positive.

In the face to face meeting with Jones, the Board were impressed to the point of being won over. He spoke confidently about his methods, relentless commitment and his self-belief in his ability to deliver success. There was not a shred of doubt that he believed he would turn things around at Stoke City and bring success to the club.

As we came to know, the *diamond* formation was central to his approach

Jones inherited Stoke City in fourteenth position in the league with thirty five points. There was a thirteen point gap to the relegation zone (which comprised the almost already doomed Ipswich on fifteen points and the weakest Bolton side in my living memory).

Jones basically had a free hit for the remainder of the season. The play-offs were just eight points away, but it soon became clear they were a pipe dream. He therefore had an extraordinarily rare opportunity. A twenty match *gimme* to plan and prepare, organise and shape the squad and embed his own brand of football.

Never in the long one hundred and fifty seven year history of the club has a manager had as long a period of preparation before a new season. Nathan was in charge for twenty one games in our 2018/19 season (including the one FA Cup match). The narrative we pretty much all accepted was that the remainder of this season was a planning phase for a successful campaign in 2019/20.

Days before Jones was appointed, we had completed the signings of Ryan Woods from Brentford and Benik Afobe (who had been at the club since the start of the season and where we had pre-agreed a large fee with Wolves). The pair cost over £15 million in transfer fees.

Before the end of his first transfer window, Danny Batth (centre half) arrived from Wolves for £3 million and Sam Vokes (Burnley's third choice combative striker) joined for an initial £8 million.

Brentford away was his first game in charge and the expectant travelling fans welcomed Jones as though he were the messiah as he crossed the pitch to take his place in the dugout for the first time.

Brentford was the only ground in the Championship where away fans could enjoy the opportunity to gather on a terraced area. For some younger fans this would be there first chance to experience that, even though it wasn't anything like the giant Boothen End at the old Victoria Ground.

Brentford interrupted the party and rushed into a 2 - 0 lead before an excellent long range strike from Afobe gave us hope and a chance to celebrate on the terracing. Brentford deservedly ran out 3 - 1 winners in the end.

I attended this fixture and after the game looked on as Jones walked back across the pitch from the dug outs, which were on the opposite side of the ground to the changing rooms. He graciously, acknowledged the fans and was no doubt pleased with their reception.

Having changed the team around we next faced Leeds United at home in midweek and produced probably the best display of the season with goals from Clucas and Allen in a 2 - 1 victory. We dared to believe!

It was false hope as three defeats in a row followed. The 2 - 0 reverse at home against Preston was disappointing and Sam Clucas missed a penalty late on. In the following game we lost at Hull City by the same margin. In this match, Sam Vokes missed *another* penalty on his debut. The hat trick of consecutive losses was inflicted at home to West Brom 1 - 0.

The next phase of the season saw us embark on a nine game unbeaten run. Winning just two and drawing seven. Jones had tightened the defence but it was at the expense of a goal threat in most games. We scored just five times in those nine games.

The first of the nine was at Wigan where we drew 0 - 0. I hadn't planned to go but news broke the day before that Gordon

Banks had passed away. Tributes came from all quarters for this masterful goalkeeper, World Cup winner and our club President. His statue was adorned with scares and messages, flowers and visits from all parts.

I regret I never saw him play and only once met him in the Waddington Suite where he was as gracious and welcoming as everyone who talks about him says. A great man who should have been knighted but for incompetence within the Civil Service to deliver that award. It should still be awarded posthumously.

The game was irrelevant really and a non-event as fans at the ground celebrated his passing with more tributes.

We moved into our last half dozen games of the season in April with an away defeat at Swansea after two sending-offs. Struggling Rotherham were the next visitors to the Bet365 where we threw away a 2 - 0 lead to end up drawing the game. After a defeat at Middlesbrough (inevitable against a Tony Pulis side) we put in a spirited performance to draw 2 - 2 with promotion chasing Norwich at home.

After a drab 0 - 0 draw at Millwall, we ended the season against already promoted Sheffield United at home. The game ended in a 2 - 2 draw against a United team who some suggested had been celebrating their promotion the night before.

Jones said after the game " We've made great inroads and I'm excited as to what we can achieve".

Jones' League statistics read like this:

Played 20
Won 3
Drew 11
Lost 6

Our league position was sixteenth with fifty five points and minus seven goal difference.

Not a single three goal haul was achieved in these twenty league games.

In the Summer Jones really went to work with shaping the squad with *his kind of players*. Gone were many established names (mostly on free transfers) and fourteen incoming players, ten signed on contracts and four on loan. Nick Powell was the pick of the new signings joining from Wigan.

We were still able to enjoy another pre-season trip to Germany, this time to the attractive Duisburg where Dan and I again met Martin and Alice at a popular bar by a large lake next to the ground. MSV Duisburg are a German League Three side. We drew 1 - 1 with Clucas neatly slotting home our equaliser.

The real business was about to begin on 3rd August at home to QPR.

Replacing Norwich, Sheffield United and Aston Villa, who were all promoted were Huddersfield, Fulham and Cardiff, all relegated from the Premier League. Huddersfield accumulated just sixteen points in their second and last Premier League campaign. Neil Warnock was also returning to the Championship after just one season with Cardiff, though he would soon exit the club during the new season.

Joining the Championship from League One were Barnsley, Charlton and of course, Nathan Jones' previous club, Luton Town.

Nathan Jones had consistently said all along that we should judge him on results in this new Championship season. The first ten games would be the barometer and fans were still hopeful, believing in Jones and the continued unwavering backing of the Board.

Game one - QPR at home

The QPR game was a car crash. Early in the game, Jack Butland raced out of his box for no discernible reason to reach a ball running tight to the by-line. His clearance, intended to keep the ball in play rather than out for a throw in, struck the oncoming QPR player and spun invitingly back toward goal for Hugill to score comfortably. Jack was still stranded out of the box when the ball entered the net.

Despite a late goal by Clucas, we lost 2 - 1. It was a very disappointing and largely self-induced result.

Game two – Charlton away

The following weekend, a glorious sunny day we travelled to newly promoted Charlton, a new ground for my son Dan and a trip to London on the train. I had visited The Valley several times in the past and particularly remember our League Cup 2nd leg there in 2000.

We had taken a 2 - 1 lead to then Premier League Charlton from the 1st Leg and held them to a 3 - 2 reverse in the ninety minutes. Extra time beckoned. We were reduced to ten men early in the first period of that extra time and feared the worst.

However we managed to equalise in the game and take the lead in the tie through an absolute thunderbolt by Icelandic, Stefan Thordardson. He picked the ball up in our half and raced up the left wing. With no other options, he cut in toward the corner of the box, still over twenty five yards out and unleashed a very special shot which crashed into the top right hand corner of the net.

The celebrations befitted the goal and despite another Charlton goal near the end of extra time, we held on to the final whistle and progressed on away goals.

I hoped for a similar result this time, without the drama. It wasn't how it played out. Charlton opened the scoring early on and Butland was again at fault. Despite a superb equaliser by Tom Ince, we went on to lose 3 - 1. The large away following, who had enjoyed the opportunity to visit the Valley for the first time in twelve years, left disappointed.

Game three - Derby at home

We earned our first point of the season in a 2 - 2 draw at home to Derby. We still needed to come from behind though after conceding in the second minute of the game.

Our on-loan striker Scott Hogan equalized after the ball deflected off him. He followed that up with another in the second half. Before and after that goal we missed two very good chances, most notably by Joe Allen from just three yards when his effort struck the post.

Derby regained parity with a penalty mid-way through the half and we couldn't find the winner despite having had twenty two shots.

Jones said in his post-match interview that "We should have six points and instead we have one. We are a good side, a really good side. We are an outstanding side outside both boxes, but in the boxes we are an average side."

My assessment is that we hadn't deserved six points, perhaps three as the performance against Derby was an improvement.

Game four – Preston away

We hoped we could repeat the type of performance against Derby sixty five miles up the M6 at Preston in midweek. Unfortunately this was not how it turned out and instead it was another unmitigated disaster. Butland was at fault for both first half goals conceded. These were basic schoolboy errors and his confidence was shot to pieces. We ended up losing 3-1 with a consolation goal by McClean making the score line slightly more respectable.

We were now bottom of the league.

Game five – Leeds at home

We were at home to a strong, confident Leeds United next. Butland was dropped and we were dismantled in the game and lost 0 - 3. Leeds dominated possession and scoring opportunities, they had twenty one shots and won comprehensively. Jones questioned the mentality of his players saying they needed to take more responsibility during games, especially after a setback.

Game six – Birmingham away

Before our sixth league game of the season we played Leeds away in the EFL Cup just three days after being soundly beaten by them on our own turf. Dan and I had been at the Oval watching an entertaining T20 Blast match between Surrey and Somerset.

Somerset collapsed from almost a hundred for no wicket after ten overs to little more than one hundred and fifty all out. Tom Banton and T20 world number one, Babar Azam dominated and appeared unmovable. It all changed rapidly and Surrey wasted no time in chasing the runs down with overs to spare.

We found a bar where we could listen to the closing stages of the cup match at Leeds, which had been going rather better than either of us expected. We had begun strongly and secured a two goal lead in the first half. As the pressure grew we crumbled in the second half. Butland was at fault for the first goal we conceded as he struck a goal kick against a Stoke defender allowing striker Nketiah to collect the ball and halve the deficit. We ended up drawing 2 – 2, sending the tie to a penalty shootout.

We listened nervously to the penalties. It was 4 – 4 in the shootout when Jack Harrison missed for Leeds. Butland stepped up to take the next spot kick and scored to win the tie. It was a brave response following the home defeat just days earlier.

In the match at Birmingham on the following Saturday, there was nothing really in the game during the first half. We took the lead after fifty eight minutes as Lindsay arrived at the back post to head in a cross from Tommy Smith. The lead lasted fifteen minutes and once Birmingham had equalized their winner followed shortly afterwards.

Jones appeared to be becoming desperate and said that he wished we hadn't scored as early in the game as we did!

Game seven – Bristol City at home

The home game against Bristol City felt like a must win game and when Clucas scored a fine goal after four minutes to give us the lead, we looked comfortable. However, Joe Allen was dismissed for a dangerous challenge with only twelve minutes on the clock and we were up against it from then with almost eighty minutes still to play.

The pressure told in the second half, albeit rather cruelly as Tom Edwards in trying to clear a goal bound effort bundled it into the net for their winner.

Game eight – Brentford away

Brentford away, a tough fixture. This is where Jones began his managerial tenure. We needed to do far better on this occasion.

It was a relatively quiet game with the hosts having the better of things without troubling the scorers. In a match where neither goal was seriously threatened, we escaped with a 0 - 0 draw.

This was only our second point of the season but still sufficient to lift us off the foot of the table, above Huddersfield.

It was now one hundred and sixty eight days since we had won a league game.

Jones said of all his continued changes, "I want to keep a settled winning team, I'd love that, but at the minute we've just got to find that formula".

Jones had already had nine months and thirty games to *find that particular formula.*

Game nine – Nottingham Forest at home

Time was really running out and we desperately needed a victory and three points. We started impressively and deservedly took the lead through a fine sharp finish from Lee Gregory.

What we had been unable to do all season was capitalise when we were on top and leading in games, especially at home, and reach a position where we built enough of a lead to make the game safe. We repeated this weakness against Forest despite dominating possession and efforts on goal.

Yet again we fell victim to another routine goalkeeping error by Butland, as he fumbled a cross, allowing Lolley to score sharply. It appeared as though all the early belief had deserted us as Forest went 3 - 1 up with two goals in fifteen second half minutes.

McClean, who possesses a Duracell battery again gave us hope with a glancing header late in the game. It was never enough to enable us to save the game.

Game ten – Huddersfield Town at home

Bottom of the table Huddersfield were the next visitors at the Bet365 for our tenth game. It was likely time had already expired for Nathan Jones and if there was ever going to be a resurgence, it had to be now.

We started this match one point and one place above the Terriers. I was in a lively coastal resort of Cascais near Lisbon on a golfing trip watching our match on my iPad. Most other people in the Irish bar were understandably more interested in watching Bayern Munich tear Spurs to shreds in a 7 – 2 victory. Not me.

Huddersfield scored after eighty two minutes in a game where we enjoyed the majority of possession but with no end product. There was a feeling of inevitability as again we misfired and looked devoid of confidence in the vital final third of the pitch.

Jones was resigned to the fact that his time had come to an end, saying "I've tried to arrest the downward spiral and I've been unable to do that" and went on to say, "The owners have stuck by me unbelievably and I'm sorry I've been unable to repay them."

We were now rock bottom of the league, six points off safety. We had secured two points in our opening ten games.

There was no way back for Jones.

Remarkably, four days after Jones had given what was essentially a resignation speech in the wake of that chastening 1 - 0 home defeat against Huddersfield, Stoke picked up their first wins of the season. These victories came in consecutive matches at Swansea and then at home to Fulham with the forty six year-old still in charge.

At Swansea we triumphed with a very late winner, scored by Hogan from a fine angle after a good downward header was won by Vokes. Then against high flying Fulham at home where we got the breaks and Tyrese Campbell gave us the lead followed by (and hold the back page) a penalty, yes a penalty scored by Lee Gregory.

Thoughts that there might be a chance for Jones to retrieve his and Stoke's position were rapidly extinguished. The next match proved a dull affair and 1 - 0 defeat at Sheffield Wednesday which was then followed by a dire performance and defeat at (Gary Rowett's) Millwall. It was well and truly over. Jones knew it, we all knew it.

Before Jones departed, he looked emotionally drained and bordering on ill. He had always been a nervous ball of energy at the best of times, it seemed even more exaggerated at Stoke and he was now a broken man.

From being bullish and full of life when he was appointed in January earlier this year, Jones sounded like a man desperate to be put out of his misery less than nine months later. He told the Stoke players on at least three separate occasions that he had taken charge of his final game.

Upon his appointment in January, Jones spoke with such conviction, intensity and confidence at the bet365 Stadium when he was presented to the media. Jones' message to supporters was "I can promise you that my staff will give them a team that they can be proud of. I guarantee it."

The Stoke board felt strongly that Jones could not have worked any harder. Leaving aside the tactics and the coaching, he tried everything with the players, from being nice to being nasty, from giving them more time with their families to getting them in training every day. All the while he chopped and changed the line-up. The end result, however, was nearly always the same. His messages, for whatever reason, never got through and failed to translate into positive results.

What Nathan Jones introduced at Luton clearly worked, but there are fundamental differences between Stoke City and Luton Town. Jones was taking the lower-league players at Luton on a journey with him, whereas the majority of the Stoke squad had already experienced the Premier League; where he wanted to go.

Some players inexplicably lost their form - Jack Butland went through a torrid time - while others appeared disillusioned.

On top of everything else was the money factor. Luton's weekly wage bill for the entire squad was £115,000. Stoke, in comparison, had eight players earning more than £40,000 a week when Jones took over.

Dealing with some of the personalities in that Stoke dressing room was never going to be easy. The overriding feeling toward the end was that Jones was out of his depth.

Jones not only persuaded the Board that he was the right man for the long term, he percolated belief throughout the majority of supporters. His style was almost evangelical, his passion and desire are undeniable but his promises to restore the glory days of our proud club were hollow.

I don't think he was intentionally spinning us all an elaborate and false line. I think he truly believed that the belief, passion, energy and collective shared vision, would deliver his and our aspirations. He was wrong. The Board were wrong. And we were ultimately wrong to be taken in by him.

His final statistics for league games are:

Played 34 games
Won 5 (15%)
Drawn 13 (38%)
Lost 17 (47%)

When Jones exited the club, we were rock bottom of the league with eight points from fifteen games. We were six points from safety and possessed a very unwelcome minus fourteen goal difference.

We also had to endure an embarrassing exit from the FA Cup at the hands of League Two, Crawley Town. It was excruciating and we lost on penalties (predictably) having taken the lead in the game through Vokes before being pegged back. In the shootout, Crawley scored all of their penalties, we managed just three from our five spot kicks.

The club and its supporters are keen to move forward. It's still quite hard to shake off the memory of this episode in our history at the hands of a delusional man who threatened our place in the Championship. Some of the opinions on the Oatcake Fanzine refer to Jones as a *fraud*, a *narcissist*, a *fantasist* and *the most catastrophic thing to hit SCFC since the gales of 1976*.

Whatever your opinion, it was an extremely damaging period from which we will eventually grow and transition away from. The scars however remain visible and now we rely on Michael O'Neill to navigate us to safety and truly restore pride in our famous football club.

CHAPTER TWELVE

Coates Family

Peter Coates was born in Goldenhill, Stoke on Trent in January 1938.

Son of a miner and the youngest of fourteen children, he regularly attended the Victoria Ground with his father. He founded Stadia Catering, specialising in servicing football grounds and after a merger with Lindley Catering he became Chairman of the company in 1968, a role which he undertook for thirty three years.

In 2000, Bet365 was founded by the Coates family with Peter's daughter, Denise, playing a leading role. Denise Coates together with her brother John are joint Chief Executives. Peter remains as Chairman of this global betting company which is the business that has contributed most significantly to the wealth of the family.

The *Sunday Times* rich list for 2019 had the Coates family in the top 20 for the first time, after adding £1.1 billion to their net worth during the year. The family are now worth approximately £7 billion, advancing to 16th in the 2020 rich list.

It was 1989 when Peter Coates became the majority shareholder of Stoke City. He remained as Chairman until 1997 and was influential in the clubs move to the Britannia Stadium, relocating from the Victoria Ground which Stoke City had occupied as its home for one hundred and nineteen years since 1878.

Unfortunately the club were relegated to the third tier of the football league in the same season. The fans protest against the board resulted in Peter Coates stepping down as Chairman, though he retained his majority shareholding.

The club was sold to a consortium of Icelandic businessmen, Stoke Holding SA, in 1999 for £3.5 million.

An interesting and turbulent period for the club followed, during which there were several new managers. The Icelandic Gudjon Thordarson was one of those, who eventually steered the club back to the second tier through the play-offs in 2002. Tony Pulis also had his first spell at the club and then there was a strange and largely enjoyable roller-coaster of a season under Johan Boskamp.

In May 2006, negotiations between Peter Coates and the Icelandic owners were concluded and he re-acquired the club once more for £1.7 million through a subsidiary of Bet365. His first appointment was to reinstall Tony Pulis as manager.

Within two years, Stoke City were promoted to the Premier League, back in the top flight for the first time since 1985.

Aged eighty two, Peter has taken a step back at Stoke in recent years and his son has taken on a more hands-on role, so much so that some would claim that John is running the club every bit as much as Tony Scholes, the chief executive.

Peter's passion for Stoke City remains strong. He rarely misses a match and is often seen at the training ground, where he has lunch in the canteen with staff and players on Fridays. You would be hard pressed to find anyone in football who has a bad word to say about Peter, including the various managers he has dismissed over the years.

The Coates family are always visible and a genuine part of the club, unlike many owners who seem entirely detached from their football clubs. This reflects their philosophy; the club isn't primarily a balance sheet asset. Peter explained in an article in the *Guardian*, "Me and my family, we don't look at Stoke as a business, for us it's something important for the area and something we want to do."

Naturally their investment decisions are always made with all the best intentions for the club, and their generosity is clear to see. Unfortunately, nothing completely guarantees that all spending decisions are successful. There is always an element of speculation.

The owners, as fans, have enjoyed their tenure especially in those Premier League years. They point to the fact that after Stoke won promotion in 2008, the only other clubs to spend the next ten seasons in the Premier League were the traditional big six and Everton. It is also a fact that Stoke were never in serious danger of being relegated until the season that they actually went down.

The spotlight remains on the club after relegation to the Championship. There has been a feeling that poor decisions which contributed to relegation have been repeated. It is inevitable that this causes supporters to start losing confidence and question the roles and accountability of everyone involved.

More than £60 million has been spent across the first three transfer windows in the Championship and new manager, Michael O'Neill has received assurances that he will continue to be able to invest in the squad.

As well as fighting a relegation campaign in their second season in the Championship, due to a woeful opening third of the season under Nathan Jones, the club also need to be very watchful of Financial Fair Play rules.

The rules governing the Championship clubs' profit and sustainability require that clubs' losses are less than £39 million over a rolling three year period. But it's far more complicated than that. Stoke City's annual accounts for the year ended May 2019 displayed a £15 million loss but with players asset value depreciated on a straight line basis over the term of their contracts, player sales can deliver a positive profit boost to mitigate losses.

For example, Stoke signed Xherdan Shaqiri for £12 million in August 2015 on a five year contract. Three years later when he joined Liverpool for £13.5 million, the profit on this sale in Stoke's accounts was c£8.7 million as his book value had reduced from the original transfer cost by 3/5ths, or 60% to £4.8 million.

At least half a dozen Championship clubs are poised to breach Financial Fair Play rules at the end of the 2019/20 season and at risk of starting the following season with a points deduction, unless they can achieve promotion to the Premier League. Several clubs had forecast player sales to balance the books. However, given the level of financial uncertainty which exists due to the Covid-19 crisis, the three year financial reporting window may be put back.

Two clubs, Derby County and Sheffield Wednesday, had executed a different financial manoeuvre by selling their stadiums to wealthy owners to offset their looming Financial Fair Play breach. Both clubs faced independent disciplinary hearings relating to these financial transactions. This culminated in Wednesday receiving a sanction of a twelve point deduction effective in the 2020/21 season for including profits on the sale of their stadium to the club owners, disguising their breach of the rules. Maybe there will be more to follow?

Despite all these financial pressures, Stoke's owners froze Season Ticket prices for the thirteenth successive year for the 2019/20 season. The cheapest adult season ticket at Stoke remains £294, equating to less than £13 per game. The average cheapest ticket price in the Premier League is a little over £600, more than double that of Stoke City.

This was a generous gesture while the club were in the Premier League, notwithstanding that revenue from match day ticket sales represent a much smaller proportion of total income. In the Championship, it's an even greater signal of their commitment to the club and its supporters. The average cheapest season ticket price elsewhere in the Championship is £340.

In addition to ticket pricing, free transport is available to all twenty three away league games for season ticket holders. I recognise that not everyone will choose to use this facility, but it is nevertheless another meaningful gesture.

The Coates family reaction to the Covid-19 Pandemic was also in sharp contrast to many other clubs, including those in the Premier League.

Stoke City were one of the very first to commit to paying all match day staff in full for postponed games in the 2019/20 season and that there would be no job losses over an uncertain Summer. Tottenham, Newcastle, Bournemouth and Norwich in the Premier League in contrast furloughed non-playing staff benefiting from the Government's scheme. Derby and Sheffield Wednesday from the Championship did the same.

Another example of the generosity of the family was the £10 million donation from the Denise Coates Foundation to the NHS. Peter said that "We wanted to do something tangible to show our support and commitment".

I appreciate that the family are extremely wealthy and can afford such a donation, but actually *doing it*, unlike the vast majority of the other multi-millionaires in the UK is what stands out.

In July 2020, Stoke City were awarded special status by the Ministry of Defence. The Gold Award is their top employer recognition award, rewarding the club's support of the Armed Forces. Stoke City are the first professional football club in England to be awarded this accolade.

I trust our owners and respect their loyalty to the club, its fans and the local community, where they are also the largest employer. Peter Coates legacy will be steeped in Stoke City history and in John and Denise I hope and believe that our club will remain in stable, strong hands for many decades to come.

CHAPTER THIRTEEN

Michael O'Neill - Welcome!

The dismissal of Nathan Jones seemed to be dragged out longer than necessary. It may well have been that planning was going on behind the scenes and it appears that was the case as O'Neill was installed on 8th November, just one week after Jones departed.

Michael O'Neill played for several clubs over a twenty year period from 1984 to 2004. His four hundred and nine appearances were with thirteen different clubs including Newcastle United, Dundee United, Hibernian and Wigan Athletic. He also earned thirty one International caps.

His most significant managerial experience comes from managing the Northern Ireland national team, which he undertook for almost nine years. He led Northern Ireland to qualification for the European Championship in 2016 in France, the first time in thirty years they had qualified for a major tournament. At this tournament, he led the side through the Group stages into the second round, losing narrowly to Wales.

Put into perspective, Northern Ireland were eliminated in the same knockout round as England. It was an amazing achievement.

O'Neill's club management experience is much more limited with his successful two-year spell at Shamrock Rovers the main highlight.

I have a slight hope that, instead of another trip to Germany in a future pre-season, it might be that we are able to travel to Dublin for a friendly against Shamrock Rovers given the connection. It would be a great location and trip for many to enjoy.

Back to the current priority. Saving Stoke City's season having been marooned at the bottom of the Championship after fifteen games.

O'Neill was appointed just one day before the crucial fixture away at Oakwell. Barnsley were just one point and one place above Stoke in the league before this game. It was clear that O'Neill appreciated the significance of the fixture and wanted to be a part of the match day preparations even though he had only been appointed hours earlier.

Game One - Barnsley Away 9th November 2019

It had been the first time we had played Barnsley since Boxing Day 2007, our amazing promotion season to the Premier League. On that occasion, Liam Lawrence scored a hat trick including two penalties in a thrilling 3 - 3 draw. Our record in the previous eighteen games, stretching back thirty one years to September 1988 was poor. The record read; nine defeats, six draws and three wins.

Barnsley had been promoted back to the Championship after a momentous promotion season where they finished second with a whopping ninety one points. The one place they sit and one point above Stoke City in the league is not a luxurious position. They are second bottom, five points off safety.

Oakwell, where Barnsley have played their football since 1888, is a good, traditional stadium. Three of its four stands are relatively modern and the view from the large away end is exceptionally good.

Barnsley town centre is more like *The land that time forgot* and on this wintery November day, it was bitterly cold. My son, Dan, and I had driven to Leeds where we were staying overnight and travelled by train between Leeds and Barnsley. It was an old two coach diesel which took an hour to cover the twenty two mile journey despite the advertised thirty five minute journey time.

There were no other football fans on the train. I guess most, if not all Barnsley fans are home grown, either born or still living within a short radius of the town. This is certainly the case with two of their most famous fans, Sir Michael Parkinson and Dickie Bird who were both born locally. Otherwise they would probably follow another of the more fashionable teams in Yorkshire. Such as Leeds or one of the Sheffield duo (probably more likely United after their return to the Premiership in 2019). Not like glory hunters such as my son and I from Northampton, following Stoke City.

I think it's fair to say that the town centre has been under invested in over several decades. A redeeming feature are the selection of welcoming, traditional public houses. Good real ale was on the menu at a shade under half the cost of a pint of Peroni in a standard London pub.

Despite Stoke's desperate start to the season now almost a third through, there was an inexplicably large away following. Four thousand fans had made the journey. The town was busy and our fellow Stoke fans who we met in the Old No 7 pub, Steve and his son Joe, all commented how strangely confident everyone following the Potters was.

In the busy away end a catchy song had been composed and was being chanted to welcome our new manager, Michael O'Neill fresh from managing the Northern Ireland national team. This was his first game in charge and by goodness we needed a new manager bounce.

The stands were filling fast (partly due to the fact that the bars had already sold out of beer) and despite our predicament, the air of positivity was very apparent.

Ahead of the game and after a briefing by the caretaker staff about the next day's trip to Barnsley, O'Neill's inclination was to leave things alone as there was hardly any time to adjust the formation significantly, especially given the time available to do so. However, playing three central defenders at Oakwell was a concern for O'Neill.

He did, at that stage intervene and with the support of the Stoke City board, he made changes when it would have been easier to do nothing and absorb what the players then served up.

Behind this decision was the push to get a result against our fellow strugglers at the foot of the table and before the international break immediately after this game. So, he changed the line-up and the system. Sometimes risks are worth taking and let's be fair, the line-up and the systems (whatever they indeed were meant to be) had failed us very badly so far in the campaign.

Come the end of the afternoon, Stoke were off the bottom of the Championship table and the travelling supporters were doing the conga behind the goal.

We started the game positively, (*this was new*) and pressed from the kick off. After just eight minutes and having already drawn a number of hurried clearances from the Barnsley defence, their goal keeper Bradley Collins advanced well out of his box to take a free kick (harshly awarded against Stephen Ward on the touch line). He scuffed the set piece and the ball reached Sam Clucas just inside our half of the pitch. The keeper was retreating to his goal in a panic because having brought the ball under control a yard inside our half of the pitch, Clucas attempted an unlikely, speculative effort to score from fifty plus yards out.

He struck the ball cleanly and it sailed high above the retreating goalkeeper. I put my arm on my son's shoulder and said to him *"can it really..."*, all we could do then was watch open mouthed as the ball kept a true line toward goal (unlike ninety nine of every one hundred efforts taken quickly from the half way line, (unless of course you were Charlie Adam for whom this type of effort was a trademark of his).

It bounced in front of the goal and entered the net, high up.

It was the perfect start.

Then all hell let loose. Within seconds, players all converged in front of the away fans (which was at the opposite end of the ground). Amazement in the audacity of the goal bound effort turned to an ecstatic celebration. The release of this moment seemed something that was such a long time coming. It was important that so many travelling fans had witnessed it.

But after all, it was just 1 - 0, we had been there many times before and with over eighty minutes of the match remaining, there was ample time in which to concede our customary two or three goals.

The reaction resulting from our wonder goal belonged to Stoke as we continued to press as before. After another incisive move McClean raced into the box. As he went past a defender on the inside he was instantly floored. Penalty surely? The referee wasted no time and pointed to the spot.

This was where euphoria soon turned to unbridled fear. For most, if not every team, the award of a penalty in their favour is an amazing bonus, of an almost certain goal. A goal which in our case would put us 2 - 0 up. Not entirely unchartered territory for us but rare indeed. And all we needed to do was score a penalty, just twelve yards out and only the goal keeper to beat.

Now. Our penalties record is a bit shoddy. When I say *shoddy,* I mean the worst of any professional team in Europe. In our previous one hundred and eight games, we have been awarded thirteen spot kicks and missed nine of those glaring chances. It became a joke in the stands. We genuinely dreaded these occasions when we should have been jumping with anticipation.

Lee Gregory accepted the challenge and stepped up. We were about as nervous as in the league cup penalty shootout at Anfield just three years earlier. He struck the ball right footed. It wasn't going right in the corner but he seemed to hit the ball cleanly enough. Fortunately, their keeper went the wrong way and ball rolled unchallenged into the net.

After a half second delay for disbelief, we again celebrated the goal in uninhibited fashion.

Before half time, we could have had a third but that didn't quite happen. Nevertheless, 2 - 0 away at half time was a rare and glorious luxury. Surely it couldn't get any better than this?

As I have said earlier, what we need now is a period of quiet stalemate for the first fifteen minutes of the second half to neutralise and take the sting out of the game. Just nothingness, with the ball hoofed into all quarters of the stands.

But this is Stoke City we are talking about and of course this didn't happen. After just moments of the restart, our defence parted as though Moses commanded it himself and a neat, albeit unchallenged finish, made it 2 - 1. All our hard work and utter domination now rested on a single goal lead that we knew could be extinguished at the drop of a hat.

Barnsley were on top now and moments later, following a tidy passing move had a good looking penalty appeal. We feared the worst but the referee waved it away and footage later confirmed he was correct. We don't always get the rub of the green in these situations, but we were grateful for it in that moment.

We regained control once again and created a few good, and one fabulous chance. We missed all these including the final opportunity that fell to Tom Ince after a subtle, perfect cross put him in a one on one situation with the goal keeper inside the six yard box. Although we all harboured thoughts of going to rue these chances, we had gained a corner from this last, exquisite opportunity, even if it was scant reward for the glorious chance that we had created and spurned.

The corner was directed toward the back post where (unusually) we had enjoyed good success in winning headers. The ball was sent back into the centre of the goalmouth. In that crowded area, Joe Allen swivelled ten yards from goal and while falling himself managed a decent connection with the ball.

The ball was struck on the ground to the goalkeepers right. It was relatively close to him but he struggled to get down to the ball and it soon nestled in the net to make it 3 - 1, right in front of us.

For those reading this who are not Stoke fans, the first thought and instinct is probably *well that's restored the two goal lead then*. For me, Dan, Steve, Joe, every other Stoke fan in the stadium that day and for Ade, Simon, T4 and the rest of the group the immediate thought was different.

While in the process of experiencing another mental celebration, the thought was, *we scored three! In one match!*

The last time we scored three goals in a game was at home to West Brom on 23rd December 2017, almost two years earlier, when we won 3 - 1. I was watching in a bar in Hong Kong, enroute to Melbourne for the Boxing Day ashes test match.

This was therefore quite a lot to take in.

As we were calmly *taking it in* the team were still pressing and in another slick move, twenty five yards out, the ball fell on the half volley to man of the match Sam Clucas. He immediately rifled a perfect shot into the very corner of the net. So, before we had finished celebrating the third goal, we had a fourth.

The last time Stoke scored four goals in a league game was December 2015, this was one hundred and fifty seven matches ago when we came from 3 - 2 behind to win that thrilling contest at Goodison Park 4 - 3. Marko Arnautovic scored the fourth goal with a scuffed penalty as he lost his balance while taking it and which still went in to secure that famous victory.

Now it was sheer party time. We could even have had a fifth when the sub Diouf, a firm favourite who had scored twenty four goals in his one hundred and forty two appearances for the club over six years, raced through toward goal. Naturally he didn't have the composure to finish, but that would have been greedy.

At the full time whistle the celebrations continued. A very large and noisy conga made its way along the front of the away stand ushered by very forgiving, if amused home stewards.

Michael O'Neill walked off humbly with some brief applause to the travelling fans.

If Nathan Jones had still been in charge and achieved this result he would have been chest thumping like a rabid WWE star in front of us. He was undoubtedly passionate. And we adore passion, drive and energy but let's face it, he was as mad as a box of frogs.

The truth is, there is no way on gods earth that Nathan would have achieved this result. Michael O'Neill had put some round pegs in round shaped holes and suddenly we all understood the formation, the pattern. It's not actually that difficult.

For the first time in a few years after attending a match, I went to bed reliving the goals. I had a smile on my face and slept soundly.

CHAPTER FOURTEEN

The rest of 2019

It had been a very successful first game, including goals, a penalty scored and three valuable points against a team with a strong record against us (who we also leapfrogged in the League).

Now for a chance to build on that at home against struggling Wigan, but also another team who for the last decade have relished league games against us.

Our last league victory came in May 2009. Since then we have drawn seven and lost three of the ten games. The last defeat was the embarrassing 3 - 0 reverse at home last season.

Many of the more recent games against Wigan had taken place in the Premier League. These include five 2 - 2 draws between the clubs.

In the dramatic televised match at the Britannia Stadium in December 2009 with the score at 1 - 1, Wigan had a free kick in their own half. In an instant Figueroa sent a low drive, as though with a one iron in golf. It was a sublime strike which sailed over the defence and goalkeeper Sorenson also stumbled back tracking as the ball entered the net for a goal of the season candidate.

Stoke restored parity in under a minute as Ryan Shawcross headed home from a quality cross by Matty Etherington. The remaining highlight was a penalty awarded controversially as Huth brought down Gomez, with almost everyone believing Gomez was in an offside position. Thomas Sorenson saved the penalty by Rodallega. This was his fifth save from the last six spot kicks against him – a stunning record very unlike our current form.

Our stand out hero from the most recent encounter at Barnsley, Sam Clucas, was missing for the Wigan clash through injury. Typical, he starts to play really well then instantly suffers an injury. He was replaced by Nick Powell, who joined from Wigan in the close season but who had made just two appearances this season, also through injury. Otherwise we were unchanged.

Fielding a substantially unchanged team and system is something we rarely if ever experienced under Nathan Jones.

The mood was positive and a good sized crowd assembled on a dismal November day. We started brightly and created a number of good early chances culminating in a header by Powell that rebounded back off the crossbar. We looked to be pretty dominant when, after another attacking move by Stoke, the ball was cleared from the edge of the Wigan box. Joe Allen attempted a clearance and miss kicked. It was still ok though as Tom Edwards was between their striker and our keeper and could hook the ball to safety.

As the ball neared our box, Jack Butland was racing out and must have called for it as Edwards left the ball. Butland made good contact but his clearance struck the approaching Edwards and looped into the air. With our keeper stranded the ball fell to the closest Wigan player who instinctively directed the ball toward our goal. It bobbled excruciatingly into the corner of the net.

Three chances to clear the danger had been squandered and we found ourselves a goal down at half time despite our pressure and dominance.

However, with the same level of performance we knew that we could still turn this around. We needed another strong performance from our wide players, especially James McClean.

McClean has attracted attention and criticism from fans across the UK for refusing to wear a poppy on his shirt.

He grew up in the Creggan area of Derry in Northern Ireland. Having represented Northern Ireland at under-21 level, he received FIFA clearance to play for the Republic of Ireland in 2012. He has since earned sixty five caps.

McClean's assertion is that the poppy stands for all of the conflicts that Britain has been involved in. This includes Northern Ireland. He maintains that if it was simply about WW1 and WW2 victims, he would wear it without a problem.

He also confirms that he would not sing the British national anthem that he asserts would be disrespectful to the place that he comes from.

As many critics also existed based solely on his performances on the pitch. He had regularly failed to mark attackers tightly enough when playing at left back and as a winger, didn't consistently take players on and deliver accurate, penetrating crosses.

Since Michael O'Neill joined the club as manager, McLean rapidly began to win over the fans.

Credit where credit is due. In the Barnsley game and even more so in this game against Wigan, he appeared a different player. Played as an out and out wide man, he attacked the opposition and delivered fabulous paced, accurate crosses.

To be fair to Stoke fans, they totally recognise his transformation and greeted his Man of the Match accolade with pleasure and enthusiasm. He would be sorely missed at Cardiff for game three of the Michael O'Neill era.

We equalised against Wigan from a free kick after another telling run by McClean which our Centre Half, Danny Batth, slid in to score in Peter Thorne fashion from a couple of yards. We were on top again now and from another McClean run and cross Ince struck a fierce shot which the keeper saved well. Ince probably struck the ball too sweetly as a yard either side would have resulted in a certain second goal.

With time ebbing away and Sam Vokes now also on up front with Mama Diouf, Vokes got a good head onto a high ball to the edge of the box. After a mix up in the centre induced by Ince's committed challenge (am I really reporting this? He never does that) the ball fell to Diouf just eight yards out. We were three minutes into added time as he stroked it into the net at the Boothen End.

A long and boisterous celebration took place, both on and off the pitch. We had secured the win at the death and continued the form shown at Barnsley to thrill the home support.

This was a seriously big moment for our club and our season. It lifted the club to twenty second place with this victory, only in the bottom three on goal difference.

We left the stadium to be greeted by rain in the dark late November afternoon, but no one cared. We had smiles on our faces and for a second weekend running would have a good Saturday night.

There was no respite though as Cardiff City away was the next fixture in just three days time as the fixtures just kept on coming.

Our trip to Cardiff was good one, the weather was fairly clear and we enjoyed our toll free ride over the Severn Bridge. Dan and I arrived in Cardiff relatively early, checked into our hotel and enjoyed a beer in the lounge. Simon was joining us. He had recently retired and was making the most of a midweek trip to a new ground (for him and Dan).

I had already visited the Cardiff City Stadium for our FA Cup 3rd round replay in 2011. In a poor game, it was John Walters who broke the deadlock in the first half of extra time. He added a second near the very end and we progressed through the rounds smoothly to reach our first ever FA Cup final in that memorable season.

On this occasion, spirits were high after recent results and we felt we were out of intensive care and in recovery mode. Cardiff had a new manager, Neil Harris who was only recently appointed and this was his first home game in charge.

It was a miserable evening weather wise and the game was also dreary. Only two moments stand out. First when Cardiff were allowed to steal fifteen yards in taking a throw in on their right flank that allowed (combined with our generous defending) Cardiff to advance into our penalty box. The ball was crossed to Bacuna who made no mistake to give the Bluebirds the lead.

In the second half we felt we should have been awarded a penalty, this time it was denied, but that's the way it goes. We enjoyed 70% possession, without making it count on the night.

Our home game against Blackburn Rovers followed on Saturday and while we battled to claw ourselves back into the game at 1 - 1, we conceded again and came away with nothing.

All the good work seemed to have been in vain as we lost away at Hull City 2 - 1 having taken the lead through a Vokes header early on. I didn't attend the game though many of the lads did and all reported how awful we played in the second half.

There was definitely work to do. We had slipped back to second bottom and still four points from safety.

We had enjoyed the new manager bounce, but had seemingly slipped back into some old ways. O'Neill expressed great displeasure at the performance at Hull and asked the players for a response at home to Luton Town in midweek.

Over the years we have enjoyed some good games against the Hatters, but none as dramatic as in September 1982. There had been many changes to the Stoke City side in that pre-season. The legendary Denis Smith departed along with Lee Chapman, top goal scorer in the previous season who joined Arsenal for £500,000 (big money in those days).

Incoming players included George Berry, who became a massive fans favourite (ooohh Georgie Berry!) also Mickey Thomas joined the club and pacey winger Mark Chamberlain (Chambo).

Chambo immediately earned rave reviews with his fierce runs down the wing and in the home game against Luton he twice beat defenders before crossing for George Berry to score with two well taken headers from close range. In between these goals Paul Walsh scored a 25 yard scorcher for Luton.

The drama continued as Peter Fox was sent off for bringing down Walsh and left the pitch in tears. New rules had been introduced that led to Foxy's sending off and he was so distraught that he threatened to quit the game entirely.

Paul Bracewell first took the keepers shirt. Brian Stein (brother of our famous Mark Stein) then equalised and following that, Derek Parkin, another of our outfield players, took over goal keeping responsibilities.

This allowed Bracewell to resume in midfield and he took advantage by giving Stoke a 3 - 2 lead. Stein promptly equalised for Luton before Mal Donaghy gave them the lead with a looping header. With ten men, Stoke themselves equalised again, this time Brendan O'Callaghan making it 4 - 4 after eighty five minutes.

More drama was to follow as Luton were awarded a last minute penalty. In a game of end to end football and goals galore. Luton could win it with the final kick of the game. Our stand in keeper was sent the wrong way by David Moss, but the ball struck the inside of the post and was cleared to safety in front of the Boothen End at the Victoria Ground.

The fans celebrated as though a famous victory had been achieved. Perhaps they were celebrating what will always be one of the most memorable games in living memory.

I didn't attend the game as my girlfriend wanted me to attend a family event. We stayed in a hotel overnight, (I don't even remember where) and I managed to get back to the room for the last minutes of match of the day. When I tuned in, our game was showing and was 3 - 3 at the time (this was before mobile phones etc. and I didn't even know the final score of the game).

The last few minutes were brilliant and harrowing at the same time and I celebrated that last ditch penalty miss as though I was in the Victoria Ground. My girlfriend was unimpressed.

Back to our 2020 fixture, and without being dominant, Stoke did something they had rarely done in the last two years. They picked off the opposition and scored three clinical goals seizing on mistakes by the Hatters. First James McClean struck from a Vokes assist to boost his growing reputation as a powerful and dangerous winger. He then provided an excellent cross after a powerful run for Joe Allen to double the lead before half time.

Not exactly new territory, but very welcome and any nerves in the ground subsided.

Any fears of a Luton comeback were extinguished just five minutes into the second half. Joe Allen pounced on hesitation in the Luton defence and coolly slotted home from the edge of the box to all but seal the win.

It proved an important win and pulled us up to three points behind Luton who were in twenty first place and just out of the relegation zone. O'Neill had surpassed the points haul of Jones in seven games. In these matches he had gathered nine points. Nathan Jones' return was eight points from fourteen games.

The matches just kept on coming and another home game against Reading followed. It was a dull game and neither side had a shot on target in a goalless stalemate. Charlie Adam played for Reading that day and was one of the best players on the pitch. I was pleased that he received a good reception, which he appreciated and was well deserved for his seven year spell at our club. He made one hundred and fifty six appearances for Stoke, easily the most of any of the eight clubs he has represented.

It was another point in the bag and the gap to Luton and twenty first place was now two points.

Our next match was away to Middlesbrough, a midweek evening fixture that was being televised by Sky on 20th December. I wasn't able to attend this game and looked forward at least to tuning in to watch the boys on TV. I have great admiration for the travelling fans on these occasions. Friday night for an 8pm kick-off in Middlesbrough isn't really an away supporters friend. It's almost impossible to get there for kick off from work and unlikely there is any chance of a pre-match beer (which is part of the normal ritual).

This felt like an important game. The loyal band of away fans were making themselves heard at the Riverside Stadium, a ground very similar to our own Bet365 stadium. We were three points behind Boro and had narrowed our goal difference deficit to minus eleven. Theirs was minus twelve. A win would take us above them and out of the bottom three in the last match before Christmas.

I was impressed with how we started the game, dominating possession and creating chances. The only thing missing was a goal that our tidy play had deserved. The goal did eventually arrive in the fifty third minute with Clucas, who had been a handful all game, scoring neatly from close range.

Given our dominance and now a goal, I felt we could and would go on and win this match. However, we held the lead for just four minutes. After the equaliser, the confidence drained from us yet again. It looked for all the world as though we should have been awarded a penalty as Clucas was clearly fouled. This was waved away and added to his and our frustration.

After they scored a second goal to take the lead, it never really seemed likely that we would recover. Where we had been clinical against Luton, we were wasteful at Boro.

So it would be Christmas lunch with the club still in the relegation zone, two points adrift.

Michael O'Neill was facing the challenge of clawing the club out of the relegation zone with an air of calmness. In utter contrast to how Jones operated, he accepts strong results with humility, knowing there is more to do. As for setbacks, he accepts them without over reacting. It feels as if he is able to relax the players in a way that Jones had never done, remaining on the level and keeping them focused.

He would need all these skills as the season progressed. Starting with a big Boxing Day fixture at home to Sheffield Wednesday.

Wednesday also faced the shadow of a Financial Fair Play charge which was hanging over them.

We started the Boxing Day game well, with good tempo and movement. A purposeful approach in the early stages which was rewarded with a goal after eleven minutes. Joe Allen tried a volley after a lapse in the Owls defence, it was blocked and from very close range McClean made sure the ball had crossed the line.

McClean, again possibly our best player sent in searching crosses one after the other. Lee Gregory was on the end of two of these but headed wide on both occasions. Good chances had yet again been squandered.

After a let off just before half time when Wednesday hit the post, a nervous half time interval followed.

In the second half, when a cross by Barry Bannon was flicked in at the near post for an equalizer, it appeared all of the good work was in vain. Things got worse after another seven minutes. Jack Butland had saved well from a Sam Winnall Header, only for Lees to nod home the rebound.

Wednesday, and their irritating manager Gary Monk, couldn't believe their luck. We huffed and puffed without any real penetration and time was ticking away. It was well into stoppage time when the ball dropped to Tyrese Campbell from a Clucas header and he acrobatically volleyed home.

With just a minute or two of added time remaining we regained possession and pressed for the winner.

I have observed this situation on many occasions. Three outcomes are possible. A magical winner with the last kick of the game in the sixth minute of injury time; a breakaway by already fortunate opposition who naturally score clinically to celebrate in front of their away fans and, most frequently, a gentle drift to an inevitable draw.

Well. Cue an amazing celebration as from a corner, won by the possessed McClean chasing down a seemingly lost cause, the ball fell to Vokes a couple of yards out and he scored gleefully in front of the Boothen End.

Even though the Boothen End wasn't completely full as a good number had headed for the exits having weighed up the unlikely odds of a winner in this situation, the relief and feeling of justice being done was huge. We had seventeen shots in the game. Sheffield Wednesday had four. It was a result worthy of a largely dominant performance.

Michael O'Neill stayed calm. He welcomed the win, the points, and looked for more progress away from the relegation zone.

This win lifted the Club out of the bottom three for the first time in the season. A startling fact. It was only on goal difference above Luton, but the lift that this gave to fans was so very apparent.

Our next fixture was away at Fulham in a congested Christmas period. It was our last match of 2019 and Fulham were in good form, especially at home. They started like a train and their movement and passing in the first half was terrifying. Thankfully, Jack Butland had returned to good form and was able to repel most of their attempts. He was beaten after almost half an hour when another slick move ended when a cross come shot from Knockaert was parried by our keeper but Decordova-Reid was on hand to score from the rebound.

In a strange game where we could easily have been 3 - 0 down by the interval, Stoke started the second half far more positively. As we went deeper into the game, it was as though Fulham were ruing their missed chances and were now content to hold on to the one goal lead they had earned. This invited Stoke forward and both Clucas and Ince went close to a equaliser.

Fulham were grateful for the full time whistle and while Stoke were narrowly beaten, there were positives to be taken from the game. We remained out of the bottom three as Luton lost at Bristol City. Just a single point separated the bottom four teams.

CHAPTER FIFTEEN

2020 A Year No one Would Ever Forget

A New Year, a new start. It's symbolic around the world. Many cultures celebrate the event in some manner and January 1st is often marked as a national holiday, as in the UK.

The New Year is often welcomed by huge firework displays across the world, perhaps the most iconic being in Sydney, where the Sydney Harbour Bridge is the centre piece for one of the most expensive displays in the world, costing upwards of £4 million.

I was lucky enough to arrive in Sydney on New Year's Eve 2017 to watch England in the final Ashes test and stayed with an old friend, Dave from Gravesend who moved there with his wife almost twenty years ago. From Balgowlah Heights, a very attractive suburb of Sydney, there is a good view of the central display in the distance featuring eight tonnes of pyrotechnics. Several other displays also take place in a sequence throughout the suburbs. It was a great sight.

Dave's advice was simple and to the point. "Stay with us, watch the display from here, it's carnage in the City, three hours of queuing for fifteen minutes of Guy Fawkes and no alcohol".

Sold. That's what we did and it was splendid!

Rivalling the Sydney display are those in Hong Kong, where stunning views across the harbour enhance the show. Also in London, where £2 million buys an amazing spectacle, set to music. It's a great sight and my view is always perfect, on a forty six inch LED TV screen at home, glass in hand with the wife, and most often a few friends.

I always recall Dave's wise comments.

In London, and widely across the UK, on the stroke of midnight a Scots language poem by Robert Burns is sung to the tune of a traditional folk song. "Auld Lang Syne". A farewell to the year that has passed.

Almost every Stoke fan was happy to do that at midnight on 31st December 2019.

Many Scottish people complain about how the words are distorted across the world, and most definitely throughout England. It's only ever the chorus that gets sung here so you would have thought that four brief lines of a verse wouldn't be too hard to master. The most common (but not only mistake) is in the last line, where commonly "For the *sake* of Auld Lang Syne" is chanted. For the record the correct words are "For Auld Lang Syne".

I was born in England, I support England and Stoke City. My Mother was Scottish though so that makes me half and half. I still get mildly irritated by this, which means that within two minutes of the New Year I already have something to moan about.

Our New Year's Day results had not always been kind and this year in 2020 we had a trip to Huddersfield Town. The Terriers were nineteenth in the league a full seven points ahead of Stoke. I have been to Huddersfield twice previously. The first time was in 1991 toward the end of the season at the old Leeds Road ground where we were soundly beaten 3 - 0.

The second and more painful visit was on 30th December 1995. It was a bitterly cold day and the stadium, the unfinished McAlpine Stadium, was open on two sides. We had taken the lead in the second half through a Mike Sheron strike.

What a striker he was and one of the best pieces of business Lou Macari ever transacted, arranging a swap for the misfiring Sheron from Norwich for our own Keith Scott. The difference between the two was that Sheron was an accomplished goal scorer and Scott was most definitely not.

The swap deal took place in mid-season, October 1995. Sheron top scored in this season with fifteen goals. Scott scored just twice for Norwich. The following season Sheron top scored again with nineteen goals and when he left Stoke for QPR for a then record transfer fee of £2.75 million, he had appeared seventy one times and scored thirty nine goals.

Back to the game at Huddersfield in 1995, which we were seeing out quite comfortably with a 1 – 0 lead. The ninety minutes had been played and the ball was knocked into our box where no Huddersfield players were present. Our Right Back controlled the ball a yard or so from the touch line, a full eight yards from our goal.

He rolled the ball for goalkeeper Prudhoe to launch up field with his right foot. Prudhoe was a Russ Abbot look alike, and a solid keeper. He approached the ball and lashed at it. There must have been a bobble as he almost missed the ball. Any half decent contact would have sent the ball away with the final whistle due at any second. His contact was the thinnest of any goal kick I have ever seen.

The angle between ball and near post was already incredibly narrow, and yet this slightest touch saw the balling rolling back behind Prudhoe dribbling excruciatingly toward goal. Prudhoe's momentum took him further forward and he was stranded as the ball slowly rolled over the line. I am not even sure it reached the net.

It was a freak incident. And given our position in the league for the first game of 2020, we most certainly did not need anything like that today.

A strong following of Stokies added to the atmosphere and despite how busy their New Year's Eve celebrations might have been, it didn't dent their vocal enthusiasm.

The enthusiasm in the stands was mirrored on the pitch as City started purposefully. What a good start needs is a goal and it looked as though it would arrive in almost every phase of the game. It arrived after fifteen minutes when Sam Vokes tapped in an intelligent pass from Nick Powell from close range. What a great way for the team to start this new year. The issue was, yet again, that a half time lead of a single goal is always a slender one.

Having not had a single shot in the first half, Huddersfield from nowhere scored twice in two second half minutes. We had dominated almost every minute of the match and yet within five minutes of the restart we were behind. I felt shattered. We had worked so hard and done so well. To be sucker punched by two quick fire goals (one an own goal) knocked the stuffing out of many Stoke fans.

Unusually, the team didn't respond as many of the fans had. Quite often in the recent past, when adversity struck, we struggled. Not on this occasion. The two early goals conceded meant over forty minutes remained in the game to rediscover the form we displayed in the first half. It was vital that we restored parity a soon as possible and that's what happened.

Just seven minutes after the body blow of conceding those two goals, Nick Powell scored confidently after a clinical cut back pass from Campbell who had advanced down the right wing. It was the least we deserved and it was clear the fans knew that. We could now confidently search for the winner.

The winning goals came from Tyrese Campbell, our young buck, finding his feet in the most confident manner possible. First, he gathered the ball and unleashed an accurate low shot that nestled into the right hand corner of the net. Then he followed this up, seizing on a weak punched clearance from the opposition goal keeper. The goalkeeper was scrambling back toward goal when Tyrese calmly lobbed the ball over him and in for the fourth and decisive goal.

It was nothing more than we deserved. Sometimes you don't get what you deserve. This time we did.

We managed the game solidly from there, though many fans were so involved in New Year goal celebrations they almost wouldn't have noticed otherwise.

We capped the game with a smart finish by substitute Lee Gregory in the final minute. It had been many years since a five goal away haul (in the league) back to the last game of the 2006 season at Brighton.

That match was played at the strange, open Withdean stadium (which was really an athletics ground). It was Johan Boskamp's final game as manager as we won convincingly 5 - 1. Adam Rooney scored a clinical hat trick and my son, Dan, was mascot. A great day.

From a position of not scoring more than three or more goals in eighty eight games before O'Neill's appointment as manager, this feat had now been achieved in four of his eleven games in charge.

Now it was only the home fans shouting abuse toward James McClean (for which they were duly punished) as Stoke City fans, in the main, recognised the contribution he was now consistently making as a winger in this league.

Our next game was a tricky FA Cup tie at Brentford. I wasn't going to go, but in the end decided to make the trip. This would be the very last opportunity to visit Griffin Park and with a welcoming pub on each corner of the ground, my local Stokie fan mates in Northampton, Garry and his son Jamie decided to go. As did Dan and I.

The league was so very much our priority, however O'Neill played a strong side. Brentford in contrast made many more changes. It was a good day out, even though we lost 1 - 0 to an in-swinging free kick from a tight angle where our excuse for a wall disintegrated in front of our eyes.

While I was initially fairly upset about how our wall had been arranged for the free kick that led to the goal, we couldn't get too excited about this cup exit. We had considerably bigger fish to fry.

Millwall at home was our next game in the league. A very resolute Gary Rowett side arrived at the Bet365 on 11th January and fought out a dour match with few goal scoring chances. Despite 60% possession we couldn't translate this into goals and had to settle for a point. Another moral victory for Rowett.

The Millwall game was on the Saturday and I left on holiday to Florida on the Sunday, a complete coincidence. My wife and I had enjoyed a few days in balmy Miami and then drove through the full extent of the Florida Keys to Key West before taking the short flight to the Bahamas. We arrived in Nassau the day before we played our next game away at West Brom.

Long gone were the days of turning up and rolling over West Brom (home and away) in the Tony Pulis era and before that under Lou Macari. Lou had the luxury of having Mark Stein in his side who netted five times in five appearances against the Baggies. Under Tony Pulis we enjoyed an amazing run of games against these local rivals.

Between 1988 and 2012 there were twenty eight matches between us. Incredibly West Brom won just once! They were utterly sick of Stoke City as I heard directly from a variety of Baggies fans who I both worked with and who were clients while I was working at Lloyds Bank.

We really did a number on West Brom in those times, and then the tide turned. They had also beaten us convincingly earlier in the season in the match between the Nathan Jones dismissal and the appointment of Michael O'Neill. Rory Delap was in charge for the 2 - 0 reverse. This away fixture was going to be a real challenge as they were closing in on automatic promotion together with Leeds United.

I found an Irish bar, Shenanigans, in Nassau who were able to show the match in their quiet bar. It was eighty five degrees outside and I was watching Stoke City in an air conditioned bar on my own.

We started brightly and not long into the first half Tyrese scored clinically after being beautifully set up by Tom Ince who did all of the hard work and selflessly squared the ball inside their box after a good run with the ball. Tyrese did the rest and was developing into the real deal for us up front.

We defended stoutly from that point and saw out a priceless single goal victory. It was also great to hear the away fans singing the old favourite "We always beat West Brom, We always beat West Brom". Magic.

I arrived home from holiday in time for the home game against Swansea City. This was Michael O'Neill's fourteenth league game in charge, equalling the same number of league games that Nathan Jones had managed the club earlier in the same season. It was also our first chance of a double over any side this season.

It was a good game, we certainly had more chances and efforts on goal, but Swansea had a large share of possession, 63%. First Allen, then Clucas, McClean and Vokes all had good efforts before Clucas broke the deadlock in the second half. He had been on the end of quite a lot of stick from the travelling Swans fans (his former club) and made a point of running the length of the pitch to celebrate his goal in front of them.

Late in the game McClean robbed Marc Guehi and was bearing down one on one with the keeper, albeit at a bit of an angle. He went for power rather than placement and thrashed the ball through the keeper for the second goal in front of the Boothen End. He reminded me of the frightening sight of Don

111

Goodman charging toward goal when playing for West Brom at the Hawthornes against Peter Fox.

A good solid win and a clean sheet were very welcome.

The Jones versus O'Neill stats for their respective fourteen games of the same season read:

Nathan Jones

Played 14
Won 2
Drew 2
Lost 10
Points 8
Goals for 13, Against 25

Michael O'Neill

Played 14
Won 7
Drew 2
Lost 5
Points 23
Goals for 23, Against 15

A stark set of statistics which reveals the extent of the transformation in all on-field departments at the club.

Sadly, O'Neill's statistics didn't improve in the following fixture away at Derby where we were comprehensively beaten 4 - 0. Wayne Rooney made important contributions including a precise curling free kick from twenty yards out.

We were back at home on 8th February against troubled Charlton Athletic. They hadn't won an away game in the league since August and were being dragged into the relegation shake up having begun the season in very good form.

We dominated this game from start to finish. It took almost half an hour for James McClean to score from close range after Powell had headed on a Clucas free kick. These three players seem to appear at heart of everything good emerging from Stoke on the pitch and were creating a good understanding.

The game didn't go entirely to plan as Charlton equalised on the stroke of half time. However, our lead was restored after just two minutes of the second half as Ince found space and slotted the ball under the keeper to make it 2 - 1. With Charlton chasing the game a fast breakaway saw Tommy Smith cross for Nick Powell to score confidently. A solid 3 – 1 victory, opening up a five point gap between us and the relegation zone.

In midweek Preston North End were the visitors and while we were in good form and indeed dominated the chances created in the match, we were sucker punched twice by an experienced Preston side. Still positive signs though as well as a dent in what had become a very positive home record.

The weekend brought another away trip and Dan and I caught an early train to London enroute to QPR.

The train from Northampton shortly after 9am takes just under an hour. It's often busy and regularly occupied by a number of Stoke fans when we are playing in the Capital. Trips to London are popular affairs with a large number of away fans, choosing public transport opposed to either the free coach travel or driving. This frees up the full day for pre-match rituals (involving beer and food) as well as post-match autopsy (involving more beer).

Joining the train service at least an hour before us in Northampton, the Stoke fans on the train had already made deep inroads into their slab of Stella Artois. Dan and I have a plan for a full English breakfast in a small cafe near Euston. The fellow Stoke fans on the train also have a plan and are likely to continue with a liquid diet.

Depending on the match day destination, London Bridge and pubs in Borough Market are a regular choice of many travelling fans. Occasionally enroute to Crystal Palace or more recently Charlton or Millwall, Dan and I also tend to gravitate to Borough Market where there is a vibrant atmosphere and countless food options. The beer is pricey, but that's London for you.

After our hearty breakfast near Euston we embarked on the Central Line journey across to Shepherds Bush. In previous years we would frequent the Bree Louise pub also close to Euston. The Bree was a fabulous venue with well over a dozen real ales and just as many real ciders on offer. Unfortunately, this multi award winning pub no longer exists and was subject to compulsory purchase so that trains can (eventually) travel between Birmingham and London less than fifteen minutes faster than at present, at a cost of over £100 billion when the HS2 project is delivered.

On this occasion we travelled straight to Shepherds Bush where we met friends Martin and his daughter Alice at a bar reserved for away fans. The last time we had seen them was in Duisburg where we shared a beer in the sunshine at the bar by the large lake, adjacent to the ground.

The bar in Shepherds Bush was an attempt to coral many away fans rather than have them appearing in pubs and bars across the area. The bar itself was fine, but it's not very inspiring. On our last visit in the previous season, we managed to gain entry to Brewdog which was quite entertaining. Most other establishments were refusing entry to away fans and demanded to inspect match tickets to give assurance that they would be only allowing home fans into their bars.

I hadn't seen Stoke either win or lose at Loftus Road despite three previous visits, two 1 - 1 draws and 0 - 0 in the fixture last year. The 1 – 1 draws came in 1997 and 2007.

In the first of these games, Graham Kavanagh gave us the lead from close range after four minutes. I celebrated fully despite being in QPR's main stand. The equalizer came from a spectacular late overhead kick scored by Trevor Sinclair. I was lucky proud to have my Dad with me at the game, one of just a few match day experiences we shared.

In the second score draw, on the final day of the 2006/7 season, we needed a win to try and reach the play-offs and were pegged back early on. Late in the game Mamady Sidibe equalized despite having a broken ancle.

In the current fixture it looked for all the world that that sequence of drawn games I had attended would be broken as Stoke scored twice either side of the half hour mark to take charge of the game.

We had started the match slowly and allowed QPR to play in and around our box with far too much ease. It all changed when Clucas picked up the ball and carried it into the area before expertly finding the corner of the net. Just a few minutes later Campbell also finished sharply after another good move.

Astonishingly, by half time it was 2 - 2. The space we continued to concede to Rangers ultimately resulted in us being punished twice in quick succession before the interval.

Powell almost regained the lead with an acrobatic effort which flew narrowly wide. After that the inevitability that Rangers would score again grew. They took the lead after seventy minutes, scoring from an angle that shouldn't have been possible with our goalkeeper, Butland, on the line. They scored again in added time to seal the win.

Our game management had been poor. Together with the away game at Derby, these were the only two occasions where O'Neill's tactics could be criticised. No one gets it right all of the time.

As we approached our next game against Cardiff at home, we were three points above a congested relegation zone. We needed to get back on track.

There was little drama. We won comfortably without really extending ourselves. Cardiff looked pedestrian and unlikely play-off candidates on that performance. An own goal and a crisp finish by Joe Allen were enough and although the gap to the bottom three remained at three points, two other teams, Middlesbrough and Huddersfield had fallen below us. We were now in nineteenth place.

We saw out a 0 - 0 draw at Blackburn in midweek with a defensive performance that Tony Pulis would have been proud of. We were missing the injured McClean but still picking up points wherever we could.

At the bottom of the table, it was becoming even more congested. Teams were also picking up points around us and we were now just a single point off the bottom three. Two points separated five teams, including Stoke from eighteenth to twenty second place. We were in the middle of this pack in twentieth place.

Dan and I were looking forward to the weekend trip to Luton where we hadn't visited for several years. In the meantime, Luton fell through the leagues and, for a period, out of the football league. Their first season back in the Championship was proving tough for them and we kicked off with Luton bottom of the table.

Steve and Joe were picking us up enroute. Steve had lived in Luton many years previously and both he and Joe have a soft spot for them. I had arranged to meet an ex colleague and friend, Justin, a Luton fan, who recommended a nearby bar with parking.

I hesitate to mention the venue as it will mean it's flooded with Stoke fans the next time we visit, but it was the Leaside Hotel, a very friendly venue where we shared a good chat with several Luton fans. We had eaten a large breakfast before leaving, which was a bit of a shame as the food on offer at the venue looked exceptionally good. Other pre match venues are thin on the ground in Luton and without my friend's advice we would never have found this one. But it was a gem.

We arrived at Kenilworth Road in just a ten minute walk from the bar and in very good time for the game. I was immediately reminded of how decrepit the ground was. Nothing had changed since we last visited years before other than it had decayed further. The view from the shallow stand (never intended for seating to be attached) was poor and further restricted if you were behind one of the posts holding the roof up.

We had imagined returning with Nathan Jones in charge of our team, Luton's ex manager which would have added to the atmosphere. As it was there was a good noise level created by both sets of fans.

The game started well and Vokes gave us a ninth minute lead turning in a blocked effort from a shot by Tommy Smith. We really should have added to that tally during the first half as we dominated the chances being created and Tom Ince in particular had an excellent opportunity just inside the box, but his shot lacked conviction and was saved.

In the second half we were sitting back too much for my liking and received a warning when Cornick was adjudged offside after he turned the ball in from a tight angle. Deep into added time a challenge in our box led to the award of a penalty. There was minimal contact and replays showed it was not a penalty, but we had given the referee a decision to make. They scored the spot kick confidently.

After the match on way back to the Leaside Hotel for a quick beer to let the traffic ease, we were astonished by the policing of away fans. First, we were held in the road outside the away end for half an hour and then dozens of police tried to channel fans away from the High Street. This was the opposite direction from the railway station where many were heading.

It was a mess and while there wasn't any trouble, if there had been it would have been as a direct result of the policing effort. We disobeyed the directions and kept to our route back to the car at the Leaside Hotel, where we met a number of the Luton fans we had chatted to prior to the game.

Our first game of March was at home to the badly wilting Hull City. Hull were in a comfortable position in the league in early January and decided to sell their best two players in the January transfer window, playmaker Jarrod Bowen (to West Ham for £22 million) and Kamil Grosicki (to West Brom for an undisclosed fee). They also suffered a number of injuries leaving the squad very weak for their remaining fixtures.

They lost to Derby and Huddersfield before a 5 - 1 defeat at home to Brentford on 1st February. It was after I watched some of that game on TV that I instantly had a £20 bet on Hull to be relegated. They were in fourteenth place and a whopping thirteen points above the relegation zone. I secured odds of 20/1.

By the time we played them at home, they had gathered two points in seven games and were in eighteenth place, just four points off the drop zone and were falling like a stone. Now it was time for us to ensure they continued that trajectory.

We absolutely hammered them. First Powell scored a header from a Tommy Smith cross, then Tyrese Campbell coolly slotted home a penalty after a handball and there was still time for Clucas to score a third before half time after a blocked effort from Campbell.

It didn't stop in the second half as Clucas scored again from a looping header. The game was already over when Hull scored a consolation, but Powell ensured the four goal margin (a truer reflection on the gap between the teams) was restored.

The only bad news was that Joe Allen was carried off with a ruptured Achilles and would not be able to play again for the remainder of the season nor represent Wales in the Euro 2020 finals.

This win meant Stoke climbed to seventeenth with forty two points. Hull had dropped to 21st now just a point from safety. My bet looked like a banker.

Little did we know that this fixture, on 7th March, would be our last before an enforced suspension of all professional sport in England due to the Covid-19 Pandemic.

CHAPTER SIXTEEN

Covid-19 and football

When I started writing chapters for this book I was thoroughly pissed off about our relegation from the Premier League and the catalogue of events and mistakes that under-pinned our decline. With our team struggling to acclimatise in the Championship and fighting another relegation battle, things couldn't possibly get worse.

Then Covid-19 struck. ......

The first human cases of Covid-19 were identified in Wuhan, China in December 2019. In retrospective studies it is believed that this new kind of SARS (severe acute respiratory syndrome) evolved in November 2019. Just as we were preparing for a regular festive period including a New Year's Eve celebration, the World Health Organisation were officially informed of the outbreak.

The first diagnosed Covid-19 cases were confirmed on 2nd January 2020 after forty one people were admitted into hospital in Wuhan. Two thirds (twenty seven) of these patients had direct exposure to Huanan Seafood Wholesale Market, which had been closed on January 1st for *remediation*.

By the time the disease was diagnosed in Europe on 24th January in France, huge swathes of Asia were already affected and the first case was recorded in the USA on Jan 20th.

The first death was reported on Jan 9th in Wuhan, a sixty one year old male with several underlying medical conditions.

As the UK's first case was confirmed on Jan 31st, cases in China had grown to over fourteen thousand with three hundred deaths. By this point, British Airways had already suspended all flights to and from mainland China.

The genie was however, out of the bottle.

By the end of February, the World Health Organisation raised the global risk of spread of Covid-19 from "high" to "very high" reporting that "this is a reality check for every government on the planet".

The seriousness of the warning from the World Health Organisation was illuminated just one week later. At this point, confirmed cases around the world exceeded one hundred thousand in over a hundred countries.

On March 11th, 2020, a global Covid-19 Pandemic was declared by the World Health Organisation. The UK Government and Bank of England acted swiftly and reduced baseline interest rate from 0.75% to 0.25% and the Chancellor, Rishi Sunak announced a £30 billion package to protect the UK economy.

By March 20th the Bank of England had reduced base rate down to its lowest *ever* level at 0.10% and the Government announced an unprecedented furlough scheme to pay 80% of wages of employees up to £2,500 per month for people who could not work. Simultaneously, the Prime Minister ordered closure of all cafes, pubs and restaurants.

The lockdown had begun in earnest.

By March 24th, 2020, global cases surpassed four hundred thousand. It had taken three months to reach one hundred thousand but just seventeen more days to escalate four fold. At this point the pandemic was out of control.

By the first week of April the death toll in Europe alone surpassed fifty thousand, while the worldwide figure was over one hundred thousand. Within two weeks the fatalities in Europe doubled.

In the UK the death toll had reached five thousand. It would also double to more than ten thousand within a week. The daily news conferences spoke about flattening the "curve" of infections and deaths to protect the capacity of the NHS. It really was a nightmare situation.

The daily death toll peaked on 21st April in the UK at one thousand, one hundred and seventy two.

By the end of May with the virus spreading across the globe in an almost uncontrollable fashion, over six million cases had been confirmed. Many highly populated countries were still early in their own curve and in the US, deaths had risen to more than one hundred thousand.

On June 15th the number of confirmed cases grew to eight million and deaths were approaching five hundred thousand. The US having by far the largest number of one hundred and twenty five thousand and other heavily populated countries such as Brazil emerging as the new epicentre.

UK Lockdown

The announcement by Boris Johnson on Friday 20th didn't come as a shock, but the reality of the situation was soon to grip the nation. Dan and I popped to our local for one last beer before that took effect and this and other establishments all closed at 10pm. It was hard to believe what was happening.

I played golf locally on a strangely quiet day on Monday 23rd. My friends, Chris and Geoff and I were due to play golf at Hunstanton on Tuesday 24th. The Spring golf trip had been taking place for over eighteen years, the March/April trip is one we always look forward to and base ourselves in the UK, or Ireland.

We had enjoyed trips to Northern Ireland at Royal County Down, Royal Portrush and Portstewart, in Scotland at various venues including Kingsbarns, Carnoustie and Trump International, Wales at Royal St David's and a variety of superb links courses in England and Ireland.

The hotel had been cancelled already but Chris and I, who live fairly locally to one another, were still pondering whether to drive to Hunstanton on the Tuesday just for the golf.

Ultimately, while taking exercise once a day was still allowed and we had played the previous day, this would have been stretching things and we decided not to travel. Golf courses formally closed on Tuesday 24th.

Despite the growing evidence and statistics, there was, for a short time, a sense of denial. The next two months told us all we needed to know and even the most fervent sceptic had to accept that we were in the centre of a unique and brutal pandemic.

The scale of this pandemic had not been witnessed by almost anyone on the planet. It led to the death of hundreds of thousands of people across the world and its intervention of normal life routines and expectations became the least of anyone's worries after it had taken hold and stripped us of so many fellow human lives.

The Coates family acted swiftly. Almost immediately the emergency income measures were implemented by the new chancellor, they guaranteed all employees of both Stoke City Football Club and of Bet365 their full salaries.

As the largest single employer in the area, this was a generous and warm hearted gesture to workers in the Potteries. It was soon followed by the £10 million donation by Denise Coates from her Trust fund to the local NHS.

At the same time, Premier League giants, Liverpool and Tottenham furloughed basic employees paying them 80% of their salaries (all reclaimed from the government) while paying their professional footballers in full - an average of £100,000 per week, per first team squad player.

They received pelters for this. And rightly so. Even Piers Morgan had an almighty public *pop* at them both, while celebrating the approach taken by the Coates family for Stoke City.

Eventually they cracked. Liverpool were the first to be publicly embarrassed sufficiently to match the gesture generously available at lowly Stoke City.

Spurs held out nearly two weeks longer. Then they committed to a two month 100% salary guarantee.

The depth of the crisis led to the realisation that a new normal way of life would be necessary. For some this might be forever.

Football eventually resumed, without fans at the matches, in the two elite leagues in England and in parts of the continent. The European Championships have been delayed a year and at least for one person that was a small blessing. Joe Allen, who suffered a serious injury in our last game before the lockdown and ought to be fit to represent his country in the tournament when it is due to be played in 2021. Provided of course it can actually take place then.

When fans do return, which they will, will we ever celebrate as we did on the packed Boothen End Terrace? Or even as we do by our seats in the Bet365? Will we squash together to get to the bar for a pre match beer as though on a rush hour tube on the Central Line?

For humans to be distanced from one another feels inherently unnatural. Giving a wide berth to others when walking, customary face masks and no shaking of hands is a new concept. Of course this is all necessary, but it feels extremely strange.

The easing of the lockdown measures in England were welcomed by the vast majority as the virus has been contained. Going back to the pub will be possible, albeit not in quite the same way.

But it's not the end. While the UK appeared to be relatively stable after the containment measures, some countries have yet to reach the peak of infections and fatalities. We are fortunate that in the UK there is a strong NHS with significant capacity. We benefit from the fiscal measures introduced by the government to protect jobs and, to a large part, the economy. Many countries still suffering the brunt of Covid-19 do not have these protections.

As lockdown eases here in the UK, the threat of a second wave of infections grows. The virus hasn't been killed. We have hidden from it, managed it where it has flared up and denied it the hosts it craves to carry and share its evil.

The thought of a widespread second lockdown is almost too gruesome to bear. The silver bullet will come in the form of a vaccine, the only question is when.

Until then it's baby steps all the way.

In the future at some point, an analysis of how the crisis was managed will take place. This will consider issues such as the UK's timing of the lockdown measures; was this introduced early enough? It will look at the availability of Personal Protective Equipment and it will review the testing and tracing capacity and capability. There *will* be lessons to be learned.

I hope that, at the same time some of the reporting in the media is subject to a similar forensic review. The apparent enthusiasm and reporting by the likes of Beth Rigby, Laura Kuennsberg and Robert Peston, seizing always on the worst possible news angle, has been ordinary at best, shameful at times.

These questions are not for now though. Plenty of time exists to undertake these 20/20 hindsight investigations and for now, continuing the fight while the war still wages, is everyone's priority.

CHAPTER SEVENTEEN

Football Returns - but not as we know it

Saturday June 20th, 2020. The day that live football returned to the Championship in England.

The Premier League had kicked off three days earlier with two outstanding fixtures to even up matches played across the division. For the next two months, it would be wall to wall televised football to complete the one hundred and ninety matches that remained across both leagues.

If someone had told me that we would be playing out the final quarter of the season in empty stadiums, with cardboard cut-out fans and canned crowd noise, I would have laughed it off. The reality is that we do not know when we will be able to return as spectators, or on what basis this might be restricted.

When Covid-19 struck, it struck hard. Between playing Hull City at home on 7th March and before the next scheduled game at Reading on 14th March, all professional football in the UK had been suspended. This was initially until 3rd April and soon extended to 30th April. It was rapidly clear that the interruption was going to be a longer one. It lasted one hundred and five days.

Our first match back was away at Reading. We had seen, from the Premier League matches that had taken place, many players were struggling with match fitness. Predicting the results would prove difficult with form out of the window.

Having purchased the package of live streams for all nine remaining games (from the compensation the club had paid to season ticket holders) we were all looking forward to the return of live football. Match day was quite different to normal, though the group of us across five separate households convened a Zoom call at 2pm, ahead of a 3pm kick off. We all opened a beer simultaneously as though together in the Fenton Bowls Club, standing in the same spot outside we had for every home game over the last 20 years. After the long enforced break this at least enabled us to view the live sport that we love.

It felt good to be underway and we all knew that Stoke City had work to do, despite our good form and results immediately prior to the lockdown.

The stream worked pretty well given how many supporters had exercised the option and were tuning in. We looked sluggish on the pitch, rusty was too kind a word. We were playing four centre halves at the back. That *ought* to make us strong in the air, but not particularly pacey or nimble.

This was exposed in the first ten minutes when Bruno Martins Indi allowed a ball played down the wing to evade him badly. It was pounced upon by the winger, crossed low into the box and tucked away neatly into the corner by Joao, Reading's Portuguese striker. There was nothing Butland could do about it.

Our one decent moment of the half was when a curling cross flew over the Reading defence. Ince appeared unmarked near the corner of the six yard box as the ball arrived to him. He struck a volley into the ground, taking a bit of sting out of the effort, which then bounced into the keeper's grateful arms. A good chance squandered.

At the other end, we felt that too many crosses were being allowed to penetrate our penalty box. Fortunately Reading also missed chances and Jack Butland made a fine save from a shot from outside the box which was heading for the corner of the net.

With five substitutes allowed in these remaining fixtures, available in three substitution breaks (and at half time), we felt this could favour us given the size and depth of our squad. Ryan Shawcross was the first player to be substituted, after tweaking a groin muscle close to half time.

It was yet another blow for Ryan. We all hoped it would only be a minor setback but Ryan's injury problems seem to recur far too frequently. It will be a sad day when he can no longer represent the club he saw into the Premier League in 2008 and captained regularly during the next twelve years. My fear is that we are approaching that point.

Both sides hit the woodwork in the second half. Reading from an excellent free kick that came back off the face of the bar. Stoke then came close to the equaliser fifteen minutes later as Campbell struck a shot from outside the box which hit the upright.

Three attacking substitutions gave Stoke more impetus as Reading appeared to tire and retreat deeper with their slender one goal advantage. Vokes, McClean and Gregory all joined the fray and McClean immediately looked dangerous on the left flank.

With the ninety minutes played we entered four minutes of added time and won a corner in the second of those. Lasse Sorensen, playing his first game since the win at Swansea in our final Premier League game two years ago, swung the corner across. The box was congested and contained all our taller players. One of those, James Chester won a header from the deep cross which he directed toward goal. Is wasn't going in as too many bodies were in the way, but the alert Nick Powell stooped to reach the ball first and guided a header into the corner of the net.

We just about deserved an equaliser, and certainly needed it as some other results were going against us. The players celebrated, leaving social distancing aside momentarily during the euphoria. The likelihood of Stoke being relegated was now 8%.

Reading will feel aggrieved, but they did precisely what we had done on the same ground in the previous season, hanging on to a one goal lead and then conceding in stoppage time as the pressure grew. What goes around comes around.

A week's break followed before our first home game of the restart at home to Middlesbrough. On Monday 23rd June, we received bad news.

Boro had sacked manager Jonathan Woodgate after their 3 - 0 reverse at home to Swansea at the weekend, plunging them into the relegation scramble. The new manager was none other than Neil (*Colin*) Warnock. He had left Cardiff in November 2019 and chose Middlesbrough in June 2020 as his next managerial position.

The universal feeling was that this would make things more difficult for us.

After three very hot days with record June weather exceeding thirty degrees Celsius, the clouds were forming on Saturday 27th as we prepared to face Middlesbrough at home, our first game back at the Bet365 since mid-March.

We started the game in 18th place in the league, on forty three points and two points of the drop zone. We finished the game still on forty three points, but now in 20th place and just a single point off the bottom three. It was a very disappointing return to home turf.

We started the game slowly which is never a good thing. Boro took the lead from a poorly defended set piece, though the scorer also did well to glance an in-swinging cross into the net. We had one excellent chance as McClean volleyed strongly from close range and their keeper pulled off a fine save. It was 1 - 0 at the break but suicidal defending near the interval almost enabled the visitors to double their lead.

Michael O'Neill was the first to get back to the changing room where it was pretty obvious he would be giving the team a dressing down. We needed to start the second half strongly.

There was an immediate reaction in the second period as we took the initiative. Three good chances were rapidly created, two to the busy McClean. After their keeper saved the first, his second effort rebounded off a post and it felt as though the equaliser would arrive.

Instead, from a Boro break, Tavernier was allowed time and space to collect a long ball, turn and create more space on the edge of the box before sending a powerful shot into the corner of the net. Jack Butland was motionless.

This was a serious blow. To cap it all, Nick Powell was sent off for two petulant challenges within a minute of each other toward the end of the game.

Neil (*Colin*) Warnock had achieved a victory in his first game in charge. Boro had won just once in fourteen games prior to this match. Relegation odds narrowed. We were now a 19% bet to go down.

Wigan away was our next game on Tuesday evening and the pressure was building.

The memory of Diouf's very late winner at home to Wigan in O'Neill's second game in charge was comprehensively erased during this, our third fixture after lockdown. From minute one to ninety we were second best, and were ripped to shreds, especially down the left side of our defence by a pacey and creative Wigan team. This weakness, stemming from the left back position was cruelly exposed and was something we had to remedy in both the short and longer term.

The opening goal came from this area, though should still have been prevented as Butland made a clumsy and unsuccessful effort to block a cross from the touch line. The ball somehow squirmed through him, struck the unlucky Shawcross on the line and was in the net. The match continued in this vein and we were fortunate to be just a single goal behind by the half time interval.

At this stage with a vigorous manager's team talk, some reorganisation and maybe a substitute or two, we hoped we could turn it around.

Once play recommenced, it was very soon apparent that this was not a possibility. Wigan scored their second, in slapstick comedy fashion, and it was clear there would be just one winner. The goal *again* from an attack down our left hand side was crossed from inside the box on the by-line. Butland got hands to the ball but only succeeded in flapping it against the bar. The ball dropped invitingly for the waiting, unmarked Wigan player in the box to tap it in.

You might think it couldn't get any worse from here. It did. Not only in terms of the score line which finished 3 - 0, but with the negative reaction of the players, who mentally folded. It was embarrassing.

With several other relegation threatened clubs gaining valuable points and sensing the possibility of their escape from the bottom three, the crisis intensified. We were now in 21st place, just a single point and one place outside of the drop zone. Our relegation odds tightened further and we were now forecast to have a 32% chance of going down.

After the victory at home to badly wilting Hull City immediately before the Covid-19 lockdown, we had climbed to a position of relative comfort. We were one of the form teams in the division. The odds on Stoke City being relegated at that stage were just 6%. Goal scoring wasn't the primary issue and even though there are some glaring gaps in our defensive line up, we felt that we had the fire power to overcome a few set-backs in games.

Since games recommenced, we had looked a shadow of our former selves. Is it because players didn't take their personal fitness regime seriously during the enforced break? Or is it that we had flattered to deceive and were not as potent as we hoped to believe?

Whatever the reason, the situation was getting serious. The performance at Wigan was devoid of a coherent plan, confidence or even desire. One of the only things that football fans cannot tolerate is lack of desire, effort and appetite for the battle on the pitch. There is just no excuse.

Given how the players performed at Wigan, they may well have been grateful that there were no supporters in the ground.

Michael O'Neill was exasperated in his post-match interview. Fans shared his frustration but were also concerned about team selections. Stephen Ward at left back could provide experience, but no pace whatsoever. This was deeply exploited at Wigan. The midfield pairing of Jordan Cousins and Jordan Thompson failed to exercise any control over the midfield area during the entire game.

In goal, Jack Butland appeared to have returned from the lockdown lacking all confidence again. The individual errors had returned at Wigan, and where Jack shared blame for the opening goal, he was fully culpable for the second. As commentator Nigel Johnson remarked, "the second goal would have been embarrassing to any pub team playing on Wolstanton Marsh Parks on a Sunday morning". It was just not good enough.

We were definitely missing Joe Allen, but needed to find a solution as he would not be available in the remaining six fixtures of the season.

A desperate performance such as that witnessed at Wigan naturally draws the attention of supporters and commentators on to the club. The attitude of the players is questioned and the manager is also scrutinised.

Supporters are understandably concerned. I am certain many shared my fear of the ultimate insult whereby our club cannot avoid relegation to the third tier of English football, (mainly due to performances under Nathan Jones, statistically the worst manager in the club's history). What would make matters even worse is if Jones, now back at Luton managed to salvage survival for Luton, currently bottom of the league. Luton proceeded to collect five points in three games including an away win at Swansea and a draw at top of the table Leeds United.

It was the perfect storm. A *shit* storm for Stoke City fans.

The morning after the game it was announced on Sky News that Wigan had entered Administration. They were the first EFL club of the season to suffer this fate and quoted the difficulties that Covid-19 has had on their revenues.

When a long established club in any of the football leagues enters Administration and is at threat of extinction, it's never a time for celebration (though I would perhaps make an exception for Coventry City). However, the intention is that Wigan complete their remaining fixtures and attract new owners as soon as possible.

The penalty for this manoeuvre is a deduction of twelve points. Wigan were comfortable on fifty points and the deduction would leave them immediately at the foot of the table, five points below Stoke and even trailing Luton Town by two points.

This single event, without a football being kicked improved the odds on a Stoke City relegation from 32% down to 18%. For Wigan, who were at a 0% chance of relegation they swept immediately to 83%, odds-on for the drop.

The twists and turns of the season continue and it remains to be seen if there will be any other similar casualties or points deductions for other Financial Fair Play breaches prior to the conclusion of the season.

Our next game is at home to Barnsley, who we overcame so joyously back in November at Oakwell. The 4 - 2 triumph on that memorable November day was Michael O'Neill's first game in charge and it was imperative he repeated the success before we embark on a formidable looking final four games, starting after the Barnsley game with Leeds United away.

On 2nd July, Hull City won against Middlesbrough and sent Stoke back into the bottom three.

The really hard work starts now.

4th July 2020, Barnsley at home

It's hard to be as passionate about a game without actually attending in person and having gone through the pre-match ritual. But it's clear from conversations with mates and right across social media that huge nervousness exists about our prospects in this game.

The general consensus was that firstly, it's most unlikely that we would keep a clean sheet, given our defensive frailties and a less than confident goalkeeper. Second, that it would be miraculous if we managed to score any more than a single goal.

The anxiety about our defensive weaknesses is understood but I felt it rather unfair to rule out the possibility we could score more than a single goal. Whatever the differing opinions, there was widespread consensus that this was a win or bust situation.

The very least we expected was an energetic start, a strong attempt to press the opposition and hopefully in the process, create and then take advantage of errors in their defence. There had been five changes to the starting line-up. They all seemed sensible. Nick Powell was restored to the starting eleven after his sending off against Middlesbrough.

The line-up looked positive and needed to be as we had only collected a single point from the three games since the return to football. Barnsley in contrast had claimed seven points and were breathing down our necks in the league table.

The early exchanges of the game instantly displayed a positive reaction. From an early corner from the right, an excellent in-swinging delivery from Clucas was brilliantly won by the busy Sam Vokes and he glanced a precise header into the far corner to give us an early lead. The relief was clear to see on the pitch, shared no doubt in locations across the UK, and elsewhere in the world by fans viewing the live stream.

Within two minutes we had repeated the pattern of the away game at Barnsley by doubling our lead. McClean chased another lost cause and when the defender sent a weak header back toward his keeper near the by-line, McClean reached the ball first and turned the ball inside where Tyrese Campbell was on hand on the edge of the six yard line to deftly back heel the ball past the keeper.

There could have been a third goal when Clucas sent a low cross in from the left and somehow the ball was cleared. We knew that a third goal would most likely kill off the game while a 2 - 0 score line meant that a single reply by Barnsley would trigger panic throughout our side.

Nerves were settled before the break as Clucas sent in a clever low corner, passing to Campbell who had peeled away from his marker and placed a precise shot past the keeper and into the far right corner of the net. We could relax and hopefully also enjoy scores from around the division as the afternoon unfolded.

The second half was relatively quiet. We protected our lead which also crucially improved our goal difference. Later in the game, Tom Ince was brought on as a second half substitute. He found space inside the box to hammer a rising left footed shot into the roof of the net and complete the victory. It was a fine finish that we had hoped to see far more frequently from Ince, hopefully it was a sign of things to come.

Our focus had always been on our own performances and results; however it was too tempting not to look in on fellow relegation threatened teams. It was good news this time as Luton collapsed to a 5 - 0 home defeat against Reading. Wigan were also defeated 3 - 0 at promotion seeking Brentford.

Elsewhere on Sunday 5th July, Middlesbrough lost at home to QPR as Colin's new manager bounce flattened. Hull also lost at West Brom.

As well as universally lifting spirits, all this elevated the club to 18th position, restored faith and belief in our players and gave significant hope that we could now escape the fear of relegation and plan sensibly for next season. But there were still five games to go, fifteen points to play for and we knew some of the fixtures were against form teams at the top of the division.

Thursday 9th July, Leeds United away

There has never been a season when this fixture could be described as straightforward. More often it's tricky, difficult or often, impossible.

Elland Road is a tough place to play any game. In our last ten matches there, we lost six, drew three and enjoyed one amazing victory 4 - 0 in 2006. In that game we dominated from start to finish with the mercurial Ricardo Fuller scoring a fourth goal to seal a magnificent, comprehensive win. Steve and Joe were at that game and Joe was lucky enough to catch the shirt thrown into the crowd by Lee Hendrie after the full time whistle.

It's been a while though. And on this occasion Leeds are deservedly on the verge of a Premier League return. They had been knocking on the door of the elite league for a few seasons, though had choked twice when in touching distance. Most felt that was not a great shame.

While they were determined to put all those disappointments behind them this time, we were desperate for points for a different, but equally desperate reason.

The opening exchanges of this game were relatively even. We conceded possession but were holding our own, without creating any clear opportunities. A draw seemed the best outcome we could hope for. It was only a minute before half time when Leeds broke down the left. The winger approached the very edge of our box and was clumsily brought down by Tommy Smith. Penalty. It was an unnecessary challenge which was set to ruin all of the good defensive work undertaken in the first half.

Naturally they scored as Jack Butland conceded for the nineteenth penalty in succession. This record goes back to New Year's Day 2014 when Leighton Baines equalised for Everton to make it 1 -1 in the 90th minute of a fixture in the Premier League.

I was there to see most of the nineteen penalties we have conceded over that period and can't remember a single occasion when Jack has got anywhere near the ball. He consistently dives the wrong way.

It had now been six long seasons since a Stoke City goalkeeper had saved a penalty (outside of a shootout). Even that, in April 2014 at Stamford Bridge against Frank Lampard didn't prevent a goal as Lampard scored from the rebound after Asmir Begovic saved the original shot. Prior to that Tommy Sorenson genuinely saved a Loic Remy penalty in a 5 - 1 reverse at Newcastle.

Tommy Sorenson remains the king of saving penalties. In just over four years from September 2009 he faced nineteen penalties as Stoke City keeper and saved seven of these, almost a 40% success rate, in stark contrast with Jack Butland's zero success rate.

Back to the Leeds match, the second half became the kind of car crash session we had experienced so many times. It felt as though we were torn between trying to regain a foothold in the game and not wanting to destroy our marginal goal difference advantage. Leeds in contrast were rampant and their relentless attacking became irresistible.

Four second half goals were conceded and despite this being a game that was a bit of a *free hit*, the 5 – 0 result was both damaging and demoralising.

Elland Road had been silent. But we had still been humbled.

This season had lingered on in a less than positive manner for far too long. We hoped to put it out of its misery, but had failed. We still had a serious task on our hands.

Sunday 12th July, Birmingham City at home

Even though the matches are coming around every few days, it's still torture in between. This is fuelled by the gravity of our situation.

Results had gone our way over the weekend, but that wouldn't be enough on its own. We needed to earn a minimum of four more points from our remaining fixtures. The home game against Blues was the stand out opportunity among our last four games.

The last three games all appeared tricky at best. Trips to Bristol City and Forest are never straightforward at the best of times and complicated this season by Forest's push for a play-off place.

In between those away games, the final home game of the season is against Brentford who were having their best season since the 1930's where they achieved three top six finishes in the top flight. This season they were in stunning form and had won all of their previous seven games, scoring nineteen times and conceding just twice. They were chasing automatic promotion to the Premier League for the first time and on current form they would not be denied. Their goal difference was forty three positive.

Brentford had won all of their games since the return to football in June.

All of this intensified the pressure on the game against Blues.

At the foot of the table eight teams were fighting to stay out of the bottom three and relegation to League One. Stoke were one place and a single point above Hull who occupied 22nd place, the final relegation berth.

Just three points separated six clubs. It was an almighty dog-fight. Birmingham themselves were three points above Stoke but they had their own troubles, they had failed to win in any of their last ten matches and recently relieved their manager of his duties. It looked as though they might fail to secure any additional points to add to their current total of forty nine and would also be in grave danger of the drop given how tight it had all become at the bottom of this relentless league.

Bright sunshine welcomed the players to the Bet365 for a 1.30pm kick-off.

Stoke started positively from the very first kick of the game. After six minutes a super cross from Nick Powell was met by Sam Vokes who powered a header onto the face of the crossbar. In the empty stadium the sound reverberated as he hooked the rebound wide.

We continued to press and both Powell and Tyrese Campbell went close as Stoke dominated. It's always vital to score when on top before the inevitable balance of play swings toward the opposition and after Powell had delivered another intelligent cross following a short corner, Centre Half Danny Batth slid in at the back post bravely and ensured the ball ended in the net. It was a crucial advantage.

We continued to press with strong attacking intent so lacking from the team earlier in the season and were unlucky not to double our lead when McClean struck a powerful shot against the bar from outside the box.

We would have taken a one goal lead at half time if offered to us before the game, but it would be a travesty to hold such a slender lead after being as dominant in this first period. Fortunately, we were rewarded late on in the half with a priceless second goal.

McClean threaded a neat pass to Clucas who found space in the box, opened his body and sent an exquisite curling shot into the top corner. It was no more than we deserved and very gratefully received. Sam Clucas, was our captain in Jack Butland's absence with a neck injury. He had a fantastic game.

Our nerves were now under control.

We managed the second half very professionally. Birmingham hardly had a sniff and the defence looked very solid. Our stand-in Keeper, Adam Davies, making his home debut acquitted himself well and kept a clean sheet.

All in all, a solid display and three magical points to lift us away from the dreaded relegation picture. It wasn't over by a long way, but this was a major step in the right direction. For Birmingham City, they face an equally nervous last three games, but without the attacking threat that we possess.

Wednesday 15th July, Bristol City away

The relentless run of fixtures continued with a trip to Ashton Gate. A tough ground to visit, though we did manage to squeeze out a 1 - 0 win there last season against the run of play. This year they are chasing a play-off place, though were a few points off that target.

We travelled to the West Country in good spirits and seeking the additional points to secure our place in the Championship for next season. With talented Brentford and the dangerous Nottingham Forest left to play the match at Bristol represents a good opportunity.

My first and only visit to Ashton Gate was in March 2000 where together with a mate and business associate (Mike the Mack) we enjoyed a strong performance by the team in an entertaining 2 - 2 draw. Strangely we were both going to be working in the area during the day! We had the better of the game where first Kyle Lightbourne and then Graham Kavanagh scored to give us a 2 - 1 lead at half time.

Bristol responded well and after they had equalised we thought we had won the game when the skilful, elegant Gunnlaugsson looked to have scored a special goal late on. That was unfortunately disallowed, but not before Mike and I had made a bit of an exhibition of ourselves, celebrating in the main stand surrounded by home fans.

We were still to meet Bristol City in the League Trophy final at Wembley in that same season, where a crowd of over 75,000 witnessed a Stoke victory in a 2 - 1 triumph. The scorers that day were Kavanagh and Peter Thorne. Thorney took his goal tally to thirty for the season in all competitions and his goal in that final was typical of his bravery in the six yard box.

What we really wanted more, despite the wonderful day out at that final at Wembley, was victory in the play-offs. This was the season we were undone by Gillingham in the two legged semi-final. I really wish I could forget that horrible evening at the Priestfield Stadium in the second leg.

The Bristol game this season was on a Wednesday early evening. I had met up with Owen, a long standing friend and Stoke City fan who was as nervous as I was about completing the job of securing our place for next season in the Championship.

While Covid-19 still gripped much of the world, a level of semi-normality was slowly resuming across the country. England had played a test match against the West Indies behind closed doors in Southampton (and lost). This was the first cricket of the Summer. Plans were also to emerge to allow fans into outdoor sports venues later in the Autumn, which gave the appearance of green shoots. However, before that was due to be implemented in October 2020, a large rise in the Covid-19 infection rate across the UK and within Europe led to a tightening rather than a relaxation of measures to restrict social distancing.

Owen and I played golf in the afternoon before the Bristol City match and arrived back at his home in Barlaston just in time for the live stream (which worked a lot better on his laptop than on my iPad). The golf was variable (as it always is). When playing with someone you have never played with on a course that is entirely new to you, my simple aim is not to look as though I have never picked up a golf club in my entire life.

For the first six holes I was utterly embarrassed. Not because of Owen's superior golf (which *was* pretty good) but by my own lack of ability. Having played championship courses throughout the UK in a semi sensible fashion, I was unable to strike the ball properly.

I had not had a drink. So my excuses were based on three things. First I had cleaned my clubs for the first time in a decade. All the grooves on the club heads came to life. But that should improve control and striking ability so it was a lame argument. Next I had only the day before taken possession of a new set of glasses. I have a prescription that's a bit complicated and perhaps that could have contributed. Third and most plausible, I was nervous about the match at 5pm.

It was the match day nerves excuse that I hung on to. If my next round of golf is as poor I will be in Happy Gilmore, club throwing territory.

As we settled down for the match the team was barely changed from the victory over Birmingham. Gregory started ahead of Campbell and with games every three days or so, there necessarily needed to be some rotation. Davies remained in goal as Jack was still suffering from a neck injury. We speculated that he may not have much of an injury and that it was a convenient excuse to enable us to stick with Davies after his performance in the game against Birmingham.

We started the game positively and it soon became an open contest with chances at both ends. While we enjoyed the lion's share of the chances, Bristol City had a glorious chance with a one on one against our keeper. Davies was off his line in an instant and before the striker was able to release a shot he bravely smothered the ball.

Gregory then had a similar opportunity at the other end but shot tamely against the advancing Bristol City goalkeeper.

On the stroke of half time, the last kick in fact, we conceded after a corner was only half cleared, Filipino Benkovic found far too much space and invitingly curled in a shot giving Davies no chance at the far post.

It was less than we deserved, but we had been becoming accustomed to that.

We started the second half brightly and Nick Powell struck the post with a fierce left footed shot. We maintained the momentum and from an excellent McClean cross Danny Batth scored a brave header diving in front of his marker. Batth had now scored in consecutive games. If his first against Birmingham was Peter Thorne esque, then the second was pure trademark Thorney. Nothing was going to stop him reaching the cross first and he headed in convincingly.

We still had chances to win the game, but toward the end played deeper to hold on to the point that would make the club almost entirely safe on fifty points.

We held out and now the chances of being relegated became a minute fraction of 1%. The relief was clear in the media, on social media and at Owen's house. We enjoyed a large pizza and a beer to celebrate in a strangely isolated table area at a local pub, obeying social distancing.

Whether we could actually enjoy the last two games of the season, is a step too far because whatever the outcome of this unique season, the rebuilding job at Stoke City remained a significant challenge.

Saturday 18th July, Brentford at home

The evening before our penultimate match, West Brom in second place in the league lost dramatically at Huddersfield. This meant that Brentford needed just a point to reach the automatic promotion places for the first time during the season. In a strange way that shifted the pressure on to Brentford ahead of their fixture with Stoke.

Our expectations were low; however Michael O'Neill had instilled a discipline and focus that had been lacking in both our dressing room and our match day performances. We had little to lose and could learn a great deal from how our team managed the significant threat that Brentford posed.

It was a generally fine July afternoon across the country. But this is Stoke on Trent. There is significant rainfall throughout the year in Stoke on Trent. Even the driest month still has a lot of rainfall. Average annual rainfall is 801mm. Average temperature is 9.2 degrees Celsius.

It's certainly not the wettest or coldest place in the UK, but on this mid-Summer day, the rain was steadily falling.

In goal, Adam Davies deservedly kept his place again despite Jack Butland's recovery to full fitness. We began the game busily. Pressing hard and man marking some skilful Brentford front men. Our pre-match conversations were about being happy to escape with a point. We looked capable of this in the early stages.

In the attacking third, Vokes was winning all the headers, Gregory was putting himself about and Clucas and Powell added creative touches.

Toward the end of the first half, another cross was won by Vokes whose header found McClean, he passed inside to Clucas who fired a low shot to the keeper's left. The ball bounced just in front of the keeper and he managed to parry the ball away, but following up was the alert Gregory who scored from close range. We had gained a precious lead which wasn't threatened before the interval.

We knew that the Bees would be throwing players forward in the second half as they searched for the goal and point to reinforce their promotion push. Our defence remained resolute throughout and though it was obvious that some players were tiring, we kept on battling.

We restricted the opposition to one goal bound effort in the second half at the very end of the game which Adam Davies, our stand in goal-keeper, dealt with expertly. In the end we managed the game well and deservedly gained the victory and three more points.

As well as defeating a very good side, we had mathematically secured our own place in the Championship for next season, after a few nervous months. Brentford's failure to win meant that Leeds United were promoted to the Premier League as Champions, ending a sixteen year absence. West Brom fans were also grateful to Stoke as they remained in poll position to secure the second automatic promotion place.

Wednesday 22nd July - Nottingham Forest away

At long last it was the final day of a gruelling and protracted season.

While we were sitting comfortably ahead of the final fixture, many other teams were sweating furiously. Forest were one of those teams.

Forest started their last fixture of the season against the Potters in fifth place. They were three points ahead of the only other team who could possibly usurp them of the final play-off place. They also benefitted from a superior goal difference of six and unless there was a significant swing during the evening, the play-offs would be a reality.

Almost any result other than a heavy home defeat would ensure that Forest would be in the shake up for a place in the Premier League. But Forest were already wobbling by the time we played them.

We started the game with nothing but pride to play for. Some senior players were rested, notably Clucas and Powell. Davies retained his place in goal after three very assured appearances.

Forest undoubtedly have talent in their squad and in Lolley, possess a winger who poses a constant threat. However, their character is questionable. Danny Batth scored the opener to give Stoke the lead. From a well worked corner he ghosted in at the back post and powerfully headed home, comfortably beating his marker. He had now scored in each of our last three games, a great return from our centre half.

Having held a deserved half time lead (ensured by accomplished saves from Adam Davies) we started the second half in search of more. However, it was Forest who scored next, an equaliser in a very similar fashion to our opening goal. Set pieces had become a fruitful opportunity for us, while remaining a problem for us defensively.

147

The onslaught that might have been predicted never materialised. Forest instead appeared to settle for their play-off securing position, and ultimately paid the price.

Instead, Stoke upped the pressure and from a low cross from Josh Tymon who had burst up the left, McClean scored from a yard to restore our lead.

Forest then folded and from a similar move Gregory scored again to increase our lead.

This might still have been enough for Forest to claim a place in the play-offs, but Stoke City, with nothing more than pride to play for, broke away in the sixth minute of added time and forced an own goal to seal a comprehensive 4 - 1 victory.

For Nottingham Forest, it was a disaster and a wretched end to their campaign. Swansea's win at Reading completed their misery. A seven goal swing occurred and Swansea finished in the play-offs while Forest had choked.

For Stoke City it was another goal fest. The only shame was that a full away following couldn't be there to celebrate and really rub salt into the wounds.

It was eventually over.

We had finished fifteenth.

What's all the fuss about!

CHAPTER EIGHTEEN

Reflections on a strange & unique season

The end of a season can invoke a variety of emotions.

Our amazing last game of the 2007/8 season where a sterile draw at home against Leicester City propelled us into the Premier League was possibly the finest celebration our club enjoyed.

At Arsenal, in the final game of our first season in the Premier League, we lost 4 – 1 but had already secured another year in the elite league. Even though I wasn't there, I know it was thoroughly enjoyed. I had a good excuse. It was my wedding day and all the group who did attend the match, joined us in our garden party the day after on a blistering hot Bank Holiday Monday.

After that we became accustomed to a relatively safe and secure end to several Premier League seasons.

This wasn't especially healthy. We grew too comfortable with our privileged surroundings.

We still enjoyed most season endings, especially in May 2015 when we comprehensively thumped Liverpool 6 - 1 in Steven Gerrard's final game. Stevie G was fortunate, it should have been nine or ten.

Two years later, despite another campaign that saw Stoke finish thirteenth, the atmosphere was markedly different. In our final home game we were trounced by Arsenal 4 - 1. We had become accustomed to turning the southern softies over at home.

This was different. The slick passing and movement of a confident Arsenal were far too much for us and after the boos at the final whistle, the ground was almost empty as the players circled the pitch.

The mood had most definitely shifted despite an entertaining win at Southampton on the final day of the same season, where Crouchy scored a good header late on to deliver us a 1 - 0 victory.

The scene at the end of the following season has already been described in this book. We won at Swansea. But it was far from enough to save us. The fabulous atmosphere in the South Wales sunshine was more akin to a wake.

Now in the Championship, the final game of our first season was strangely upbeat.

We drew against already promoted (and almost certainly hungover) Sheffield United. It was a good game which we drew 2 - 2. There was a feeling of positivity as many fans still believed the Nathan Jones narrative. The truth was that we had won once in our final eleven games of that season.

In the latest protracted and now completed season, we had secured our safety far more comfortably than it looked at Christmas, when we were bottom of the table. The 4 – 1 victory at Nottingham Forest exceeded even the most optimistic Stoke fan's expectations.

We had discovered a new hero, a manager who organised, motivated and stirred an underperforming squad into life.

In perspective, MON gathered forty eight points from thirty one games. That in itself would have been enough to keep Stoke in the Championship, disregarding the points haul from Nathan Jones's fourteen match tenure earlier in the season.

The inevitable comparison between MON and Jones statistics during the season makes stark reading. A more balanced comparison is to include the twenty games that Jones also managed in the second half of the previous season in the championship.

So here they are:

Nathan Jones

Played 34
Won 5 (15% win rate. One win per 6.5 games)
Drew 13
Lost 16 (47% lose rate. One loss every 2 games)
Points 28 (0.8 points per game)

MON

Played 31
Won 14 (45% win rate. One win per 2.2 games)
Drew 6
Lost 11 (35% lose rate. One loss per 2.8 games)
Points 48 (1.5 points per game)

There isn't a version of the stats that shines a positive light on Nathan Jones' contribution.

As an aside, MON's goal difference across his thirty one games was plus eight. During Jones thirty four games, the aggregate goal difference was minus eighteen.

I don't need to emphasise the gulf between the two any further.

Stoke city finished in fifteenth position.

At the end of the season we lost Charlton Athletic, Wigan Athletic and Hull City. All relegated from the championship to League One.

Charlton blew up in the second half of the season and fell at the very last hurdle. Wigan were relegated due to a twelve point deduction that they could not overcome as the club fell into Administration and Hull City were basically, crap. In hindsight I should have held my bet that Hull would be relegated at 20/1, rather than electing to cash-out when the season was suspended. It was a great bet though and I still made a useful profit.

Travelling in the other direction to the land of milk and honey were Leeds United and West Brom in the two automatic promotion places. They both thoroughly deserved their chance in the Premier League. The table doesn't lie after forty six gruelling fixtures.

Accompanying them in the elite league is Fulham, promoted through the play-offs. Fulham defeated Brentford in the play-off final and despite all their momentum toward the end of the season, Brentford stumbled at the critical moment.

We would be joined from League One by Wycombe Wanderers, the Chair Boys whose victory in the play-offs sent them up. Rotherham United, The Millers, also earned a return to the Championship. Welcome to you both.

League One champions were Coventry City. The ground-less, nomadic Midlands team (who were awarded the league title when the season was suspended and eventually curtailed). We shall play them at St Andrews which they will be occupying for a second season.

To me they are about as welcome as Gianelli Imbula would be on a Stoke City squad team building event.

We also welcome the three relegated teams from the Premier League. Norwich finished bottom on twenty one points and were officially relegated several games before the end of the season. The Canaries didn't spend wildly after their promotion a year earlier and will be a force next time around if they can keep the squad together.

Second bottom were Watford. I initially didn't want Watford to be relegated as I was hoping that the Happy Hammers might become embroiled in it. However, Watford chose to relieve manager Nigel Pearson with two games of the season remaining. He enjoyed just twenty two games in charge, during which time he had collected a very respectable twenty six points and dragged the club up the table from bottom of the league when he arrived in December 2019.

It was their fourth managerial change of the season and Watford have become well known for a rapid turnover of managers during the last few years.

After five years in the top flight they would now face a battle in the Championship and given their liking to change things up, I anticipate further movements at the club. I don't see them tearing up the league.

The final team relegated were AFC Bournemouth also after a five year stay.

No Stoke City fans I know are shedding any tears over Bournemouth's decline. Their tactics, endorsed by media favourite Eddie Howe, have been nothing short of shameful. Against Stoke in several fixtures they have often been the better team. However, their constant diving, time wasting and persistent efforts to get opposing players booked and sent off took gamesmanship to a whole new level.

I hope that their experience in the Championship is painful and that before too long they are restored to a more fitting environment, League One. Eddie Howe has already parted company with the club.

So it all starts again on September 12th, just fifty two days after the final league fixtures were completed.

My advice? Hold on to your hats. It's going to be a bumpy ride.

CHAPTER NINETEEN

The Future

Within sixteen days of the end of the season, preparations for the 2020/21 campaign were already underway in earnest. The players returned to training on 7th August before a pre-season fixture in Northern Ireland, at Linfield a week later.

The 2019/20 season was one every Stoke City fan was happy to consign to the history books. For the club, its management, coaching staff and players it's business as usual now with little time to waste before the new season begins.

With Covid-19 restrictions still in place, there wasn't an opportunity for fans to attend the match at Linfield. This was a great shame as it deprived us of a trip and overnight in Belfast, a fabulous City. Stoke won the friendly 1 – 0 having fielded a young side together with the returning Benik Afobe making an appearance up front.

Off the field there had been a significant level of activity. Four new players were signed in a ten day period.

The first was Morgan Fox, a Left Back out of contract at Sheffield Wednesday. The promising twenty six year old fills a position at Stoke where there had been an obvious gap. It was a weakness that we had now hopefully addressed with a specialist in that position.

Hot on the heels of that signing, James Chester was recruited on a permanent deal having spent thirteen games on loan at the club at the end of last season. He is a very experienced Centre Half and while his early performances for the club were disappointing, he certainly improved toward the end of the campaign as his fitness deepened. This coincided with a sharp upturn in results.

We already have a good selection of strikers at Stoke. Tyrese Campbell, Sam Vokes and Lee Gregory together with the returning Benik Afobe, back after a loan period at Bristol City. However, this didn't stop the club adding to the firepower as Steven Fletcher was signed whose contract at Sheffield Wednesday had expired.

Fletcher, aged thirty three, is a very experienced striker. He signed for Sunderland for £12 million in 2012, has thirty three Scotland caps and has scored one hundred and forty times over his career. Thirteen of these goals came in thirty appearances at Wednesday last season.

Our expectation is that one or other of our existing strikers will have to make way. While the signing of Fletcher felt like sensible business adding experience to the squad in true O'Neill fashion, the activity was not over.

On 17th August, Stoke made a further signing, this time it was John Obi Mikel. The thirty three year old defensive midfielder brings additional quality and experience to the club. He enjoyed eleven years at Chelsea earlier in his career where he arrived as an eighteen year old in 2006 and made three hundred and seventy appearances.

There will doubtless be some departures from the club to follow Stephen Ward and Mame Biram Diouf. Diouf was at Stoke for six years and scored twenty five times in one hundred and fifty seven appearances. We wish Mame all the best and thank him for his commitment and entertainment over the years.

Our exiled players, particularly Wimmer, Ndiaye and Etebo will probably be loaned out again unless there is an opportunity to sell.

There could also be some other notable departures, such as Jack Butland whose wretched form meant that he was dropped toward the end of the season. Transfer speculation has surrounded Jack since our relegation from the Premier League.

The excitement is already building ahead of a new season that got underway on 12th September. Before that further friendlies took place and also the first round of the EFL Cup. Stoke drew Blackpool at home being played two weeks before the start of the League season. It's effectively part of the pre-season preparations, getting the squad up to match fitness but also a genuinely competitive match with a place in Round Two of the cup up for stake.

We fielded a strong side and despite some neat passing moves, the sharpness was missing from our play. Blackpool looked like a handy side and gave as good as they got. We had good opportunities to break the deadlock, none more so than when a pass was threaded through to Sam Clucas who advanced in a one on one situation. Clucas looked as if walking in treacle and was crowded out before being able to release a shot.

The full time whistle signalled a penalty shootout. There are no replays nor extra time in this season's EFL Cup. The contest was held at The Boothen End a deserted, silent bank of red and white seats where our most fervent supporters are normally housed. James McClean took the first spot kick which was saved. Blackpool, with the chance to take the initiative, also had their first penalty saved.

Adam Davies who retained his place in goal for the Potters made a fine save and repeated that feat once more in the shootout to help Stoke to a 5 – 4 victory and a place in the next round of the cup. Not especially convincing, but progress nevertheless.

With the formal start date of the new season looming, O'Neill has the job of selecting his preferred starting eleven. It won't be an easy task, but it's essential that he identifies a successful formula and establish some rhythm to avoid the disastrous start of the previous season.

Our first half dozen fixtures appear manageable. Our opening match was away at Millwall where we were would welcomed to a silent New Den. Bristol City at home followed and after that a trip to Preston North End.

After a home game against Birmingham City, we were away at Nathan Jones' Luton Town, then Barnsley at home completes the early set of matches.

After a long period of nervousness and negativity I, just like many Stoke City fans are genuinely looking forward to the new challenge with MON at our helm.

Continuing fears of a second wave of Covid-19 cases mean that fans are denied the opportunity to attend football stadia at the start of the season. This includes the Premier League, all three EFL divisions and National Leagues North and South. Below these six tiers fans will be allowed back into football grounds provided social distancing standards are maintained. Groups of a maximum of six people can spectate together.

I fear for a large number of EFL clubs. The Premier League are largely shielded and insured by TV revenues. The Championship also benefits from meaningful TV and sponsorship opportunities. However, this may still not be sufficient to protect all of the clubs within it.

For EFL Leagues One and Two the situation is far more precarious. Clubs are expected to resume and fulfil their League and Cup fixtures with all of the costs associated with doing so, but with a relatively small proportion of the expected income.

It feels like a matter of time before we lose several long established clubs forever.

In the absence of an approved vaccine to combat and protect against Covid-19, it's hard to see the light at the end of the tunnel. There are growing concerns across many European countries, the USA and South America. This means that after nine long months and massive fiscal measures worldwide, the planet is still not in control of its destiny.

The affect on football and other sport is devastating but pales into insignificance in the face of the humanitarian catastrophe. Yet we crave the return to a level of normality and in an attempt to hang on to that, allow versions of elite sport to recommence and continue watching helplessly on our own or in small groups on TV and on other devices.

The sporting calendar is relentless. While major events such as the Olympic Games and European Championships have been delayed, the ambition is to fulfil these eagerly awaited international competitions and resume the scheduled, congested sporting calendar ad infinitum.

I would love to believe that we can shake off the fear and dangers of the Covid-19 pandemic. The reality is more likely to be a legacy that can't be sealed and consigned to history in a neat and tidy fashion.

For now we continue to hope and believe in progress. To resume what we consider to be a pattern of normal living that we had become accustomed to.

I observe mankind's adaptability, its agility imagination and above all else, its resilience.

We will resume our customary routines.

We will return to the Fenton Bowls Club for pre-match beer and banter.

We will restart the season on 12th September 2020 and despite Stoke City's illuminating form over the latter games of the previous season, we will fail to win our opening fixture against Millwall.

It has been eleven years since we managed an opening day victory, against Burnley at home, 2 – 0.

Normality will resume, in a Stoke City kind of way.

CHAPTER TWENTY

The End. For now.......

It feels as though Stoke City's chapter of footballing purgatory is nearing an end.

For the last few years going to the match wasn't as magic as it had been. Meeting the lads, enjoying the banter and having a beer were by far the best bits.

We even joked about staying in the bowling club instead of going to the match, but that would never happen. It's what we do. It's who we are.

Everyone eventually admitted the extent of the rebuilding work required at Stoke. We had made several critical mistakes. We had a job on our hands. There was no consensus about how to regenerate. And no one dared try to fully appreciate the depth of issues facing our proud club.

It all felt that it would be more difficult to solve than Brexit. The truth is Brexit was solved in less time, but the legacy remains.

However small the steps are, if they in the right direction, we have a chance. That's what I see and feel right now. Michael O'Neill has brought a level of focus, stability and results. He has saved us from the cliff edge that would have meant League One football. Instead he found goal scorers within the squad, heroes in midfield and even reached a point when fans voted for James McClean to be our player of the season. A transformation indeed.

Rome wasn't built in a day. But a *part* of it was.

That's what's happening here. It won't be complete for a long time. There will be many more setbacks and disappointments.

But we will prevail and once again step forward proudly, just like we remember so fondly so often during our decade in the Premier League.

Just like we felt when we won at Wembley in 1992, in 2000 and most famously in 1972.

We have always had heroes.

Sometimes goal scoring wizards like Jimmy Greenhoff, Mark Stein, Peter Thorne, Ricardo Fuller and Peter Crouch.

Sometimes midfield magicians like Alan Hudson, Howard Kendall and Steven Nzonzi.

Sometimes the best goalkeepers in the world like Gordon Banks (rest his soul) and Peter Shilton.

Sometimes battling defenders like Denis Smith, Steve Bould, Vince Overson, Abdoulaye Faye, Robert Huth and Ryan Shawcross.

All we ask is one thing. That they are prepared to die for the cause.

We still have heroes. Even though they are different now. The game is different now. *Life* is different now.

When they pull on the red and white striped shirt, they can all be heroes. They have a responsibility.

Some appear to understand that more than others.

For those that embrace that responsibility and return the love and affection we show them, despite the massive gulf in their personal wealth relative to most fans, they will forever be revered.

Every generation will embrace a new group of heroes to help deliver our aspirations and sometimes exceed our wildest dreams.

But it's a fragile and short lived existence, just like life itself. The wonderful, gifted, magical, sometimes *brutish* heroes of one era will come and go.

Some things don't change though. We, the fans remain resolute. And when we are no more, more fans, often family and friends pick up the mantel, the baton, and run the next leg of the eternal match. It's a relay that never ends.

When my dad passed away I found a short note in his wallet addressed to my brother John and me. We both wept and embraced. At the end of the note it simply said:

"Remember the good times we had".

We *must* remember the good times. They are the moments we should fall asleep thinking of. We cannot pretend that there weren't tough times and impossible situations either.

Without the struggles, the adversity and the setbacks *the good times* would never be so memorable.

We'll be with you, every step along the way. We'll be with you, by your side we'll always stay.

The best football anthem *ever*.

Befitting of the oldest football league club on the planet. No fan of any other club in the world has a family tree like ours. Stretching back one hundred and fifty seven years since 1863. When it all began.

We have a tradition to continue.

VIS UNITA FORTIOR

EPILOGUE

Part 1

2020 was a unique year, a unique season. Nothing we can do will enable it to be erased, despite our deepest desire to do so.

Covid-19 has taught mankind several lessons. We will learn them, studiously. But we will still not be fully prepared for the next potential extinction level event that will inevitably occur, one day.

How we prepare, defend ourselves and win the future battles is born through what we have already faced. Isn't that what evolution is all about?

By standing together, working together, *fighting together* we *will* find a way.

Briefly, during the Covid-19 national lockdown, the sight of people sleeping rough in Towns and Cities across the UK was extinguished. Sadly, this has now returned as the temporary measures to take homeless people from our streets have ended.

It proved there was a way. It took a Pandemic to stimulate the action (however temporary), but it can be done.

It should be a National priority to eliminate homelessness. One day it will become one of the most important objectives for Local Authorities throughout the UK, and be matched by adequate long term, sustainable funding provision.

That day is not here yet.

Even when it is, there will be considerable planning and work to create the housing provision. It will take years to execute the plans.

The UK's record of delivering housing provision on a scale that meets demand, especially for the most vulnerable in our society, is desperately poor. There has not been a *single year* in last seventy five where housing creation was equal to the growing demand – infact the jaws continue to widen, exacerbating the problem, year on year.

That's why Charities such as the Macari Foundation are so desperately needed. By purchasing this book you have supported that Charity and I sincerely thank you all.

EPILOGUE

Part 2 – The very end, *you have my word*

There were times when I found it difficult to write about a period that wasn't the proudest in our club's history, but it is the truth nevertheless.

Many people ask me if I will write another book. A lighter, brighter story.

It's the wrong question.

There will definitely *be* another book. But it may not be written by me.

I hope whoever writes it can enjoy painting the picture of Stoke City's promotion back to the Premier League, writing about amazing cup runs and trips into Europe. I hope they can report that we have banished our recent record at Arsenal and won at Old Trafford, repeating the victories we achieved at those clubs in 1976 (1 – 0 at Old Trafford) and 1981 (1 – 0 at Highbury).

It just may take some time.

****

The new season has commenced.

We look stronger. Despite failing (*predictably*) to win our opening game at Millwall, but we earned a point and kept a clean sheet.

166

In just over a month we have played nine times, including four EFL cup games. In those cup matches, which propelled us to the Quarter Finals for the eighth time in the competition's sixty year history, we have not conceded a single goal.

First at home to Blackpool, who we surpassed on penalties (*yes penalties*) after a 0 – 0 draw. Then much more notably away at Wolves where we fielded a young side, resting several first team regulars. We deservedly triumphed against very strong opposition and produced a second half display that had me wishing I was in the stadium to enjoy and celebrate.

Against Gillingham at home in round three, we again triumphed 1 – 0 and then met Aston Villa in Round Four at Villa Park. In a very assured display we repeated the 1 – 0 scoreline. Within a week of this game, Villa dismantled Liverpool 7 – 1 in the Premier League also at Villa Park.

The Quarter Final brings a strong Tottenham Hotspurs to the Bet365 and an opportunity to watch Gareth Bale once again in a Spurs shirt. Hopefully we can repeat the heroics we grew accustomed to when we were in the Premier League ourselves.

In the league we inevitably did concede our first goals of the season at home to Bristol City in a 2 – 0 defeat. Importantly we bounced back to win 1 – 0 at Preston. After a draw at home to Birmingham our next opponents were Luton Town, under the stewardship of Nathan Jones. We achieved a comprehensive and satisfying 2 – 0 victory to earn our eighth point of the season.

I gave my word this would be the end. But the trouble with words are that *you never know whose mouth they've been in.*

I *will* keep my word and stop right here, satisfied in the knowledge that we are on the right track.

We are ready for a rebound – hopefully a big one!

Brian's first book, *Glory Hunter* was published in Summer 2017 and briefly became the Number One best seller on Amazon in August of that year. The book also raised funds for the Macari Foundation and remains available on Amazon.

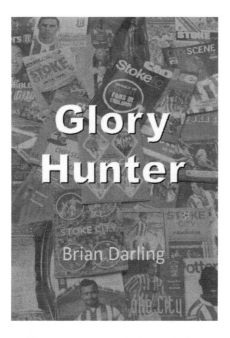

***Glory Hunter* by Brian Darling**

When Brian's ex-wife warned him not to come back from the Play Off final in Cardiff saying it was the best day of his life; he didn't. But it almost was.

As a self confessed glory hunter and lifetime fan of Stoke City, Brian has combined this passion with a career in banking.

From Hartlepool to Exeter he has made every trip and through grief, despair and heartache, Stoke City have occupied the Premier League for a decade.

It wasn't always like that as Brian's story, spanning five decades, describes. Follow his emotional journey.

169

Printed in Poland
by Amazon Fulfillment
Poland Sp. z o.o., Wrocław

63521966R00101